TOWARDS
ZERO
CONFLICT

BEGINS WITH YOU

AMYN DAHYA

British Cataloguing in Publication Data
Dahya, Amyn 1957-
Towards Zero Conflict

ISBN 1-9044281-1-8

1. Self Development 2. Motivation 3. Philosophy 4. Title.

Production: Empowered Living Publications

First Printing September 2003

10987654321
EMPOWERED LIVING PUBLICATIONS
Pol. Industrial, Segunda Fase, 72BIS, Alhaurin de la Torre,
Malaga, CP 29130 - Spain

Cover and layout by bioprana@teleline.es (Rafael Barea)

All names used in the stories in this book are fictitious and are not
intended to represent any actual person or persons.

Dear Jenny,
May you be blessed with
fulfillment of all your
dreams. Best wishes & love

DEDICATION

[signature]

This book is dedicated to all those who seek to
make this world a better place, by consciously
working towards eliminating internal and external
conflict, at all levels of human existence – a goal
that can be achieved through simple conscience.

TABLE OF CONTENTS

DEDICATION iii

ACKNOWLEDGEMENTS vii

ABOUT TOWARDS ZERO CONFLICT viii
    How to Use this Book xiii

A TRIBUTE TO MOUNT TEIDE xvi

CHAPTER 1 — DIMENSIONS OF CONFLICT 1
    The Journey up Mount Teide 2
    Seeds of Resolution 12

CHAPTER 2 — ESSENCE AND FORM 15
    Reaching for a Distant Star 17
    The Secret of Sight 22
    The Pulse of Life 28
    Seeds of Resolution 33

CHAPTER 3 — HARNESSING THE PRESENT .37
    Carving Destiny 41
    Seeds of Resolution 47

CHAPTER 4 — THE POWER OF FLOW 51
    The Flowing River 54
    The Power of Pure Potential 55
    Flowing Uphill 57
    The Waterfall 58
    The Wisdom of Alice 61
    Seeds of Resolution 63

CHAPTER 5 — THE NEUTRAL ZONE 67
    The Martian Project 69

The Visit to Harvard 77
Seeds of Resolution 85

CHAPTER 6 — EVOLUTION 89
The Promise of the Rose 91
The Spanish Bodega 95
Seeds of Resolution 98

CHAPTER 7 — EXPECTATIONS 101
The Mirage 102
The Athlete 107
Seeds of Resolution 110

CHAPTER 8 — MOTIVATIONS 113
The Coliseum 114
Seeds of Resolution 134

CHAPTER 9 — FEAR 137
The Parable of the Slave 139
The Dying Son 147
Overcoming Fear 150
Being Fearless 151
The Fatimid Fort 152
Seeds of Resolution 156

CHAPTER 10 — OPPRESSION 159
The Corporate Raider 163
Seeds of Resolution 176

CHAPTER 11 — THE COURTHOUSE 179
The Miner's Son 181
The Mombasa Café 186
Seeds of Resolution 192
An Inspired Message from a Rose About Judgement . . .193

CHAPTER 12 — JEALOUSY 197
  The Fallen Star 201
  Seeds of Resolution 209

CHAPTER 13 — SEXUALITY 215
  Strengthening Love through Meditation 217
  Closing the Void of Rejection 221
  Overcoming Lust Desires 224
  Seeds of Resolution 227

CHAPTER 14 — BELIEFS 231
  The Sparrow and the Dove 234
  Seeds of Resolution 243

CHAPTER 15 — INTERNALISATION AND TESTING OF FELLINGS 247
  Testing our Feelings 248
  Meditation of Inner Cleansing 293
  Seeds of Resolution 296

CHAPTER 16 — ONENESS 299
  The Sixty-Six Steps 301
  Meditation, an Invaluable Tool 316
  Meditation of Oneness 317
  Seeds of Resolution 321

CHAPTER 17 — HARMONY 325
  Seeds of Resolution 332
  Meditation of the Orchestra 332

TOWARDS ZERO CONFLICT AUDIO TOOLS 338

ABOUT THE AUTHOR 339

BOOKS AND LECTURES BY AMYN DAHYA 340

ACKNOWLEDGEMENTS

Towards Zero Conflict has been conceived through a team effort, based upon tireless contribution from a number of people.

In particular, I wish to recognise with gratitude, the support of my wife Karima, and children, Adil, Aly, Raheena and Noorin. True accomplishment manifests when one's efforts are nurtured by love, care and dedication.

In addition, I also wish to convey special thanks to all the members of the production team, including Diana Douglas, Arif Esmail, Zahra Datoo, Aliya Esmail and Rafael Barea.

Now begins a special journey for our readers, which we hope will culminate in the achievement of peace, harmony and fulfilment at a personal, familial, communal, national and international level.

ABOUT TOWARDS ZERO CONFLICT

*"Conflict... is like a virus that
breeds and multiplies,
infecting all that comes in its way..."*

Our Swissair flight from Johannesburg landed in Zurich at 8.00 am on a bright sunny morning in September 2000. This was a special day for my wife, Karima, and myself as we had just completed a very successful lecture tour in South Africa, where we shared the teachings from my first book, *Reflections from the Origin* and also my second book, *Parables from the Origin*, with an audience residing in a country that was going through a phase of healing from the bitter days of apartheid.

In the penultimate lecture of the tour, I spoke about the elements that make up a human being as being equivalent to the various instruments of an orchestra. I explained that when all these instruments play in complete harmony, we experience the music of perfection, at which point we gain an understanding of the true meaning of 'equilibrium' at a physical, mental, emotional and spiritual level. This is the level of *'zero conflict'*. At this level, we are able to fully harness our limitless potential. Naturally, even if only one of the instruments in the orchestra plays out of tune, the music of perfection is lost. If most of the instruments in the orchestra play out of tune, there is utter chaos. In such a state, no accomplishment can ever be achieved. Conflict disrupts harmony. Therefore, completely eliminating our inner conflicts is the key to realising our true potential, where we can experience happiness, success and fulfilment at all levels of our material lives, as well as, in our timeless spiritual journey.

As we sipped our coffee in the Zurich airport lounge, while we awaited our connecting flight to Tenerife, Karima mentioned that she had spoken individually to a number of people after the lecture and many had asked a common question, "How does one achieve *zero conflict* whilst living in a world that is ridden with conflict?" As I reflected upon this question, I was inspired with a special thought.

I said to Karima, "The importance of this question should not be underestimated. In fact, I will write a book about it!" The Universe must have been listening to me since no sooner had we boarded our connecting flight, I felt a powerful urge to write. I took a notebook out of my briefcase and began to write. The inspirations flowed through me with ease, revealing a multitude of dimensions of our inner conflicts, together with practical solutions to overcome them. The inspirations continued to flow for the next seven days. I could not stop writing. I cancelled all my business engagements in order to participate in the birth of a book, *Towards Zero Conflict*, that I believe will help bring peace and happiness in the lives of many all around the world.

Although the writing of this book was completed within seven days, it took almost three years before it could find its way into the wider world. Why was this so? In the year 2000, our family life took a dramatic turn in the direction of pure conflict. In 1998, we had lost our life's work in a hostile take over of our company. In the year 2000, we were faced with lawsuits that had been filed by the people who had taken over our company, in pursuit of whatever else they could collect from the company's directors, officers, accountants, lawyers and insurers. The whole process unfolded before us in a brutal, and a merciless manner, followed by hurtful and

damaging accusations levelled at every possible target
connected with the company.

During the two years that this legal nightmare lasted, I gained
a first hand experience of how fear can be used as a weapon to
break down the weak; how pieces of unrelated information can be
cleverly put together to fabricate an ugly 'truth' that quickly
influences people's perceptions; how far removed perceptions can
be from reality; how accusations can grow into judgements in
people's minds; how anger and hatred can destroy long standing
friendships and familial ties; how ego can manifest and consume
all that comes in its way; how greed can soar above basic human
values; how extortion can occur under the guise of the law; and
much more! No textbook or lecture could have taught me so
vividly about how conflict breeds like a virus, spreading and
infecting all that comes in its way.

At the same time, mercifully, I also gained first hand
experience of how love and unity brings power and strength to
withstand the storms created by the architects of conflict; how
faith brings strength and courage in the face of adversity; how
true friendships are discovered amidst trying times; and how
permanent bonds of love are built in the hearts of tempests.

Through these events, each and every chapter of *Towards Zero
Conflict* manifested into a real life experience for me, for which, I
am grateful, for only when one has been in fire can one
understand and explain heat. Only when one has come close to
drowning can one understand survival and the value of every
moment of life. Only when one has felt and experienced the
soothing and guiding hand of faith can one truly talk about inner
guidance. Only when one has erred can one appreciate and spread

wisdom. Only when one has experienced true love, unity and friendship can one understand their permanence. Only when one has felt the pains of breaking out of the pupa can one appreciate the wings and the elation that goes with the freedom.

It is truly amazing that, whilst *Towards Zero Conflict*, a book that is a living lesson in itself, awaited its journey into the world, I went through a personal transformation that gave me the necessary tools to teach its essential lessons, at a time when the world is troubled with so much turmoil and conflict.

As I watched the television pictures of the many millions of people around the world demonstrating against the war in Iraq, I realised with joy that humanity has been endowed with the will to overcome conflict through peaceful means. Sadly though, on this occasion, their voices were not heard and the war went ahead. However, I am absolutely convinced that these demonstrations were not held in vain, for they most certainly awakened the human spirit to unite and embark on a journey *towards zero conflict*. Hence, this book could not have made its debut at a better time!

Since inner conflicts form the foundation of external conflicts, we can actually begin to reduce conflict in this world through the simple step of identifying and overcoming our own inner conflicts. As we overcome our inner conflicts, we will become happier and better people, at an individual, communal, national and international level. When people talk of making the world a better place, it is not a meaningless or motherhood statement. We *can* create a better world for us and for the future generations by embarking on a personal journey today that takes us *towards zero conflict*.

HOW TO USE THIS BOOK

Towards Zero Conflict has been written in a simple manner that can be understood by people of all ages and walks of life. It is an invaluable practical tool with which we can recognise our inner conflicts and work proactively towards overcoming them. The teachings of this book are offered in a soft and gentle form that creates inner learning, which finds a permanent place in the mind of the reader.

Each chapter begins with an introduction to the subject matter. This is followed by one or several captivating stories that convey the individual concepts to the reader in greater depth. In my opinion, this method of learning is highly effective since the reader is fully engaged by the messages of the stories, allowing him or her to draw interpretations at a personal level. One may draw superficial messages from the various stories or search very deeply into their essence. It is a matter of timing and personal choice.

Each one of us embodies a broad range of conflicts. We are aware of some of our conflicts and unaware of others. Sometimes, we may understandably choose not to accept the presence of some of our conflicts, because admitting our weaknesses can be a hurtful or an embarrassing process. Therefore, it is important to undertake this process of self-evaluation and understanding in a setting of complete privacy. Towards Zero Conflict provides a tool for such private learning, where you need not be afraid about being completely honest with yourself. You may find that certain chapters of the book will have a greater impact on you than others, depending upon the conflicts that you harbour from within, or depending upon the conflicts that surround you.

At the end of each chapter are Seeds of Resolution, which will help you to deal with, and allow you to rise above your inner conflicts. These seeds are valuable personal development tools that will bring inner harmony, which, in turn, will result in the creation of a positive atmosphere in your daily life, from work, to relationships, to your own inner self. The Seeds of Resolution are special words that should be repeated over and over, whilst focusing on their meaning (essence). You may memorise them, if you wish, and then repeat them in your mind, with your eyes closed. These seeds are pure and positive meditative thoughts, which gradually embed themselves into the mind as you contemplate them frequently. Later, they manifest in the form of new and healthy attitudes, actions and outlook towards different aspects of your life. You may work with the Seeds of Resolution at any time of the day, wherever you may be.

At the end of each chapter, a space is provided to record your inner reflections with respect to what you have learnt. I would recommend that you revisit each chapter from time to time, because by doing so, you will derive new and deeper meanings each time. Space is also provided at the end of each chapter to record your reflections when you re-read the book after one year. Hopefully, if you have internalised and benefited from the lessons presented in this book, you will find that your future reflections will be different. This will provide you with an opportunity to monitor your progress on the path *towards zero conflict.*

This book also contains a number of simple, yet effective meditations that can be practiced regularly to assist you with the process of inner conflict resolution. Audio tapes and CDs entitled, *Towards Zero Conflict – Seeds of Resolution and Meditations,* are available separately, which contain voice recordings of the Seeds of Resolution and the guided meditations. These audio recordings serve as valuable tools for achieving greater learning from each contemplation and meditation, as they permit you to focus fully on their essence. Please visit www.amyndahya.com or see the penultimate pages of this book for further details.

A TRIBUTE TO MOUNT TEIDE

M ount Teide is a unique and majestic mountain located on the island of Tenerife in Spain. Being the tallest mountain in the Canary Islands, Teide has been recognised as a landmark by voyagers who travelled across the Atlantic since ancient times. It has a small, well defined peak, in the shape of a perfect conical pyramid, which was formed during a volcanic eruption many years ago. Ascending the mountain, the landscape changes from grass to trees to dense forests to deserts to lava rocks and snow at certain times of the year. Beautiful little rivers and natural springs carve their way down the mountain to the magnificent Atlantic Ocean. Mount Teide is endowed with beauties and mystical energies rarely found anywhere else in the world. It is at the foot of this beautiful mountain, in a little village called Las Cuevas (a Spanish word for "The Caves"), where *Towards Zero Conflict* was completed, through waves of inspiration that delivered this special book in a mere seven days!

Chapter 1

DIMENSIONS OF CONFLICT

"Conflict is a state of mind..."

Conflict has many dimensions, some of which are easily recognisable and some not. The following story illustrates how conflict resides within and around us, spreading like wildfire, if given a chance. The story also reveals how weak and vulnerable conflict can be, for it can be extinguished by simple thought.

The Journey up Mount Teide
"Conflict is a state of mind..."

One bright Sunday morning, two sixteen-year-old boys, Peter and Abdul started their journey up the great Teide. The two boys were close friends and enjoyed each other's company. Peter came from a devout Christian background and Abdul was a modern-day Muslim. Both boys studied at a British independent school, set in the heart of a Spanish-speaking community. Peter and Abdul enjoyed living in the midst of a variety of cultures. They loved nature and also enjoyed debating and searching for deep, philosophical meanings that could be found in simple little things. In fact, they loved to argue with each other about anything and everything!

Peter said to Abdul, "I watched the news last night and saw how those Islamic terrorists blew up an office building in Oklahoma City. It was horrible! The building was torn apart and so many people were injured or killed. Abdul, you are a Muslim. Tell me, why do your people like to do such things?"

Abdul, who was not pleased with the question replied, "Peter, I watched the news too and I felt very sad to see the devastation. The newscaster said that Islamic terrorists were suspected of having committed the atrocity, even though no one had been caught nor had anyone claimed responsibility. How do we know that it was Islamic terrorists who did that? Whoever these people are, they are ruthless and dangerous. But, branding them as Islamic, Christian or Jewish terrorists is not fair."

Peter replied, "Yes Abdul, I was hasty in jumping to the conclusion that it was the work of Islamic terrorists. I was quick to believe the opinions of the newscasters. I am sorry to have branded you and your fellow Muslims as terrorists. I should have known better, for I have learned much from your father about peace and compassion. I apologise for making that remark. But, I still wonder why anyone would want to do such a thing?"

Abdul replied, "It is conflict that causes people to commit such acts. These people, who we call sick, actually live in pure conflict, which causes them to express their feelings through acts of terrorism. You see, Peter, conflict exists in all of us, but in Oklahoma City, we witnessed its most extreme expression. The tragic part is that so many lives were lost in the process. This may breed anger, hatred and fear amongst the families and friends of the victims, which in turn will create new conflicts."

Peter in his usual understanding way said, "Conflict is a bad thing. It is like a virus. It breeds, multiplies and spreads, infecting all those that come in its way! Until today, I had never really thought about conflict. I have heard the word many times, but it never really meant much to me. I often associated the word conflict with war or battle. But, Abdul, you have raised an interesting point about how terrorists live in a state of pure conflict in their minds. So, conflict can also be a state of mind, can't it?"

Abdul replied, "I am not an expert on these matters but I do believe that conflict is purely a state of mind. It is something that causes us to take a negative view towards people, situations, events and everything. I mean, things like anger, greed, jealousy, frustration, hatred and revenge are all negative and destructive elements that fuel conflict in so many different directions. These elements make us focus on the bad or dark side of things. Conflict resides in our minds and if we let it grow without control, it brings out the worst in us."

Peter then said, "You see Abdul, conflict always starts somewhere. It is born and it spreads. For example, I know you don't like to talk about this, but think about Yasmin, the girl of your dreams. You would do anything for her, wouldn't you? But the harder you try to win her love, the further away she pushes you. Then, there is that little weasel Sam, who is half her size, horizontally challenged and ugly, and he gets to go out with her! Doesn't that make you mad?"

Poor Abdul, who cared for Yasmin so much, had to agree with his friend. He said, "I have liked Yasmin since the time we were in kindergarten. Sometimes, I feel that because I push too hard, she gets scared and backs away. As much as I like to call Sam a weasel, he is not one. He is not a bad person. But, there are times when I get very angry because I feel that he is stealing the most precious thing in my life. I have often resisted the temptation of decorating his round little face with two black eyes! But, what good would that do? It would breed conflict between him and me, as well as between Yasmin and me. Then, who knows, Yasmin might never be my friend again!"

Peter then said, "Oh yes, and don't forget Sam's big brother who looks like a three-hundred-pound gorilla. He would make mashed potatoes out of you!"

Abdul replied, "Then my brother Samir would take on his brother, and can you imagine what would happen?"

Peter remarked, "You see, conflict can spread very fast. Soon, our parents would get involved and who knows where it would all end up? We would all be mad at each other for a very long time! I wonder if the people who blew up the Oklahoma City building were actually ordinary kids like you and me at one time. I wonder if they allowed conflict to grow and spread within and around them."

Abdul replied, "Of course they were kids like you and me, but there must have been circumstances in their lives that gave birth to their conflicts. Peter, you and I have been taught how to avoid conflict. Unfortunately, these people did not have the good fortune of recognising this. Whilst each conflict in their lives may have started on a small scale, they allowed it to escalate into a raging forest fire, which in turn brought catastrophe to those poor victims on the TV. Is it fair that so many innocent people had to die because these individuals allowed their conflicts to spiral out of control?"

Peter remarked, "You see Abdul, it is not always easy to understand the plight of the terrorists. They may have been born and raised under injustice or oppression. They and their families may have been subjected to violence at a tender age. They may have had nowhere to turn to, nor have had anyone to hear their grievances. I really do believe that no one is born a killer or a terrorist. People become terrorists as a result of conflicts, sometimes of their own making and sometimes for reasons beyond their control."

Peter continued, "However, the good news is that conflict is a state of mind. So we should be able to erase it if we choose to, because it is not real. From what I can see, conflict reminds me of the science class in which Mr. Dorkus taught us about atomic fission. One atom splits into two, which then split into four, then sixteen, and so on."

With a frown on his face, Abdul commented, "I wish you wouldn't call Mr. Currie a 'Dorkus'. He is a great teacher. While you obviously weren't totally attentive in class — it was nuclear fission we learned about, not atomic fission — though you are right about the numbers growing exponentially."

Peter replied, "Same difference! But, my point is that conflict multiplies itself very quickly, on an exponential scale. That is probably why nuclear weapons work so well!"

Abdul then said, "You see Peter, even though conflict can spread quickly, it can also be stopped just as easily if one acts in time. If you end conflict at its source, how can it multiply? If I love Yasmin and keep trying to win her over with my love, rather than resorting to physical violence with Sam, then our brothers and parents would not need to get involved and this conflict would fail to escalate. So, Peter, I am the master of my own conflicts. I have power over them. I can stop them with a simple thought!"

Peter replied, "But that simple thought is very difficult to accept because every bone in your body wants to have that weasel Sam taken out of your way permanently! Yet, you are right, because if you can control your emotions and thoughts, then your conflicts die."

Abdul and Peter continued their climb up the beautiful Mount Teide. They were both silent for a while, reflecting upon their conversation, which was a powerful one for 16-year-olds. However, since both of them came from families where higher thinking was always encouraged, their view of the world was very different from most boys of their age.

After a while they came to a fast-moving stream that flowed into a large pond of water where its speed was completely lost. They decided to take a short break, fascinated by this phenomenon.

Peter said, "This stream flows so fast and yet after it has merged into the pond, it becomes completely quiet. That is interesting. It reminds me of our conversation about conflict. As you said Abdul, conflict is a state of mind. Therefore, it is internal. You can stop it with the way you think and the way you view everything. Here, this stream is like another dimension of conflict, which is external. It flows with a rage that erodes all the little things that come in its path. But then, as it enters the pond, it goes quiet. The conflict ends there. What do you make of that?"

Abdul replied, "My father often talks about *mass consciousness.* I like that expression. It sounds cool and intellectual!"

Peter interjected, "I am not kidding Abdul, and this is serious!"

Abdul replied, "Well, you see, the fast-flowing stream represents conflict that is external. It lives outside of the mind and it is growing through the actions of other people. It is gaining momentum. If it is allowed to continue, it could become a huge waterfall, like the Niagara Falls. But, instead, it enters the pond, where mass consciousnesses, or the collective thoughts of all people, are against conflict. Therefore, it loses its momentum and dies down. It becomes still. So, conflict can also be ended by mass consciousness."

Peter then said, "That reminds me of the movie about the life of Mahatma Gandhi, in which the angry Indians wanted to fight and kill the British. They were like the stream, growing rapidly in conflict. Yet, the thin, little Gandhi brought about a shift in mass consciousness to non-violence. He caused the stream to come to a standstill in a lake (of consciousness). The British tried very hard to provoke the Indians into a conflict, but the Indians steadfastly resolved to avoid any kind of violence. In the end, through a peaceful process, the Indians — and non-violence — won!"

Abdul, who was impressed with his friend's observation said, "Yes Peter, conflict can be eliminated simply by the way people think, either individually or as a group."

The boys walked along the pond, which had become completely still at that point. Here, the water was pure and crystal clear. It reflected everything like a beautiful mirror. Abdul looked at the pond and saw the perfect reflection of his face in it. He continued, "Look at my reflection in the pond, Peter. When the water has become completely still, it has reached *zero conflict*. Now I can see my own face in it. Wonderful isn't it?"

Peter agreed, "Yes, Abdul, when the water is not calm, you cannot see yourself in it. Yet, once it stands still, you can see everything. It is like a treasure box that opens itself up to you!"

The two boys continued with their climb up the Teide. They crossed the barren lava rock fields, where nothing grew. Abdul pointed out, "Peter, can you imagine that at one time, this entire area was molten lava? It must have been spectacular! The lava must have flowed with serious rage, to form these huge boulders."

Peter replied, "Yes, it must have been spectacular. It must have looked like pure conflict, a very long way away from the *zero conflict* in the pond! It is not surprising that nothing grows here anymore. Around the pond, there were trees, flowers, birds and everything. There was life. Yet here, there is nothing. It is barren. Nothing can grow from pure conflict."

Finally the boys reached the peak of the Teide. They marvelled at the three hundred and sixty degree view of the island of Tenerife. They could also see the neighbouring islands of Gran Canaria and La Palma. Abdul said to Peter, "It is truly beautiful here, isn't it? There is a special sense of peace here. I feel like I am on top of the world!"

Peter replied, "I felt like I was on top of the world when I saw my reflection in the pond."

Abdul remarked, "You see Peter, we have both found the top of the world but in two different places, even though we both saw the same things and places on our journey up the Teide. Yet, you are right and so am I. If we can respect that, how can there be any conflict?"

Both the boys looked down at the barren lava fields. Peter said, "That's what we must learn to avoid, for in the midst of conflict, nothing can ever grow."

Then they looked at the ocean glittering in the sunshine and at the beautiful island of La Palma in the distance, standing amidst the waves like a majestic symbol of tranquillity. With a smile on his face, Abdul said, "That's what we must learn to discover."

––––––––––––

From the story of Peter and Abdul, we learn that conflict is a state of mind. It exists internally in our minds and externally through events and the actions of others. Conflict can be very powerful because it can spread quickly, given the right fuel. Yet, it can be equally weak, because we can eliminate conflict by simple thought and consciousness.

The subsequent chapters in this book cover practical ways of developing our thoughts and consciousness in a manner that leads us *towards zero conflict*, helping us to discover peace, happiness and fulfilment by relegating our daily pressures, stresses and negative emotions to a back seat. In the absence of these pressures and worries, we can think with clarity and solve our problems successfully. While solving problems is an important aspect of living, the greater dimension of our lives lies in discovering life itself, because life, in fact, is an exalted destiny. As we discover the wonders of life, we will be able to discover ourselves, which will lead us to enrichment, growth and success at all levels of our existence.

As we all learn about *zero conflict* and try to live our lives in accordance with this "state of being," the world will become a better place, for us and for the future generations. As the famous saying goes, "A thousand-mile journey starts with a single step." Let this book represent that first step in our lives, which will lead us through a journey of peace, fulfilment and self-discovery that we all deserve. Remember Peter's words, "Conflict is like a virus. It breeds, multiplies and spreads, infecting all that comes in its way." Just as conflict has the power to spread and grow, so does *zero conflict*. Hence, the thousand-mile journey can be accomplished a lot quicker than we all think!

Seeds of Resolution

❀ Let us take a few moments to contemplate, repeat and internalise the words:

"CONFLICT IS A STATE OF MIND"

❀ These words serve to remind us that we have power over our conflicts.

❀ They reinforce within us the belief that we can play an important role in eliminating conflict, both internally and externally.

❀ Each one of us holds the key to bringing peace to ourselves and to the world at large.

My Reflections

Now   date: / /   .

My Reflections

One Year Hence   date: / / .

Chapter 2

ESSENCE
AND FORM

*"There is no such thing
as a bad person..."*

Essence and form are words that we have all heard at some time in our lives, in varying contexts. These two words describe the fundamental basis of our existence. When we look around us, we see people, plants, trees, birds, animals, oceans, rivers, buildings and so much more. Everything our eyes can perceive has a three-dimensional form, which is typically defined by length, width and height or depth. Form is also characterised by physical parameters such as weight, density, shape, colour and texture. From the moment we awake to the time we go to bed, our eyes take in a myriad of images of all the forms of everything that we have seen during the course of the day. These forms find their place in our minds, in many different ways. They stand out as singular forms (e.g. objects) or as combinations of forms (e.g. landscapes), which are perceived as pictures and images. We attach feelings, thoughts and interpretations to these images and pictures, which then manifest in our minds as perceptions and experiences. Form is everything that we can see, touch and feel. It is the only reality that we know in our material world.

What then is essence and where does it exist? Essence is the unseen element, which gives life and character to the form. Essence is intangible and yet, its presence can be felt in everything. Form is temporary and limited to time and space. In contrast, essence is unlimited and infinite. Without essence, the form disintegrates and ceases to exist. This is true for everything that we see around us in our material world.

Take for example, a patient by the name of Charles, who is on a life-support system and the doctors are frantically trying to revive his heart, which has ceased to function. At 10.59 p.m., he is alive. One minute later, at 11 p.m., he is pronounced dead. What did he have at 10.59 p.m. that he did not have at 11 p.m.? The answer is essence. We human beings, find it easier to understand and explain the things that are visible to our eyes. The invisible elements, however, are sometimes more difficult to comprehend. The following short stories explain the relationship between essence and form in a simple and easy-to-understand manner.

Reaching for a Distant Star

There was once a merchant named Chin who lived in Mongolia. From humble beginnings as a child, Chin worked hard to build up a successful enterprise in which he traded gemstones and jewellery with merchants from all over the world. He travelled far and wide in his sailboat in search of the world's rarest gemstones and metals. People respected him for the quality and rarity of his merchandise.

One day, as Chin sailed from Shanghai towards Africa, he saw a brilliant star shining in the sky. The star stood out like a diamond in the universe, giving off a radiance that he had never seen before. To Chin, this was a gemstone of the distant skies. He said to himself, "This is the rarest diamond I have ever seen. It must be enormous, for it is so far away and yet I can see it so clearly! How can I get my hands on it? How can I reach out into the skies and bring back this diamond of the universe?"

Although a much travelled man, land and sea were the only modes of travel that Chin knew. Yet, on this moonlit night, his heart and soul urged him to fly up into the skies to capture a star! Throughout his life, Chin had been a practical person. He viewed life with pure logic. He bought his merchandise shrewdly from people in distant lands, whose language he could neither understand nor speak. No challenge was too great for Chin, and he always accomplished everything that he set out to do, because his goals were practical and achievable. He worked extremely hard to get what he wanted.

Yet now, in the midst of the calm ocean, he stood on the deck of his boat, contemplating the impossible, a journey into the universe to capture this radiant star. Whilst he knew this was not practical, his heart yearned for him to do so. Physically, this was a goal that could never be achieved. He knew that only too well. But on this dark night, in the middle of the ocean, Chin could only contemplate one thing — to bring home a star!

He cried out to the star, "Oh, beautiful diamond of the universe, where is your home? How can I come to you? How can I bring you back to my home?"

The star replied, "Oh, Chin, the greatest merchant on earth, why do you seek that which you cannot reach? I am the diamond of the universe and my home is too far away for any man to reach. So, my dear friend, be on your way to Africa and seek the diamonds of the earth, which you can trade with merchants from everywhere on earth."

Chin replied, "Oh, diamond of the universe, I have looked at many a diamond on earth, but you are different. You are not like the diamonds I know."

The star replied, "What difference do you see between me and the diamonds of the earth? Is it just that I am bigger? Or am I brighter? How do you know that I am a diamond at all?"

Chin replied, "I do not know who or what you are. You look to me like the most brilliant diamond I have ever seen. You have the shape and radiance of a stone that can only live in heaven."

The star then said, "In heaven I was born and in heaven I live. But I am a star that is a beacon in the universe, for travellers who traverse the skies, the waters and the land. Tell me, Chin, what do you see in my *form*?"

Chin replied, "Everything I have seen on earth has a definite *form*. I can tell the size and shape of all the things that I can see with much accuracy. But you, diamond of the universe, are different. I see you, but I cannot tell your true size or shape. I cannot tell whether you are a rock, a diamond or just a speck of light. While I think you have a *form*, because I can see you, I cannot tell what you really are."

The star replied, "Chin, you have learned all your life to recognise and study the *form* of everything. This skill has enabled you to find, buy and sell the most unique stones and metals on earth. Your eye for detail has been your key to success. Your eye for recognising and knowing the *form* has been your greatest asset. But now, when you look at me, you are no longer sure of my *form*. You know you cannot travel to me; yet, you want to get to me. What is it about my *form* that makes you want to do this?"

Chin replied, "Oh diamond of the universe, you have a *form* that I do not understand. I know you have a *form*, but it is a *form* that has no definite size or shape. You exist in dimensions that I do not know. Yet, there is something about you I cannot see that draws me to you."

The star replied, "Chin, you are right. My *form* is flexible and fluid. I have no shape or size. There is an aspect of me that is unseen, which draws you to me. This aspect, which resides in every *form*, is called *essence*. *Essence* is the soul, energy and beauty that gives life and character to every *form*. So, Chin, for the first time in your life, you are experiencing *essence*. And of all places, you have found it in a distant star in the universe! Chin, look around you. In every *form* that you can see resides an *essence* of the unseen. If you take away the *essence*, the *form* dies. It loses its beauty, life, energy, everything."

Chin, who was intrigued with everything that he had heard, looked at the star in awe. Then, his eyes drifted to the silver waves in the ocean that shone in the moonlight. The waves danced playfully and glittered as they reflected the soft, gentle moonlight. He then heard the star say, "Look at the way the waves dance. Look at how they reflect the moonlight. Think about what makes them dance. Can you see the *essence* that causes them to dance?"

Chin replied, "No, I cannot see the *essence* that causes the waves to dance, but I know it exists. It is beautiful."

The star continued, "Once the *essence* is gone, the wave is no longer a wave. The *form* is no longer a *form*. You must learn to recognise this aspect in everything that you encounter from hereon. You have learned a great deal, Chin, from a star so far away that you do not know nor understand. Seek to understand that your world has *essence* and *form* in everything. As a merchant, you have profited from the *form*. Discovering the *essence* will now make you the richest person on earth. Not rich in wealth from the *form* but rich in wealth of the *essence*."

Four weeks later, Chin arrived in Africa. As he set foot on the shore, the trees, the land, everything he could see looked different to him. Every object had a vibrancy that he had never sensed before. A tree was no longer just a tree. It was life. It was pure energy. It was alive! Chin's eyes had been transformed forever by a distant star. He had now learnt to see the *essence* that underlies every *form*. The world had now changed for him, permanently.

In the skies, he heard the distant voice of the star say to him, "Chin, wait till you can see the *essence* of Chin himself. Then you will be able to reach out into the universe and come to get me. I will be here waiting for that blessed moment..."

This short story tells us much about *form* and *essence*. While Chin was very familiar with *form*, he knew little about the unseen element that resides in every *form*, which is its *essence*. When we think about *essence*, we contemplate concepts of life energy, spirit, soul and other unseen elements, which evoke special feelings within us. Physical aspects of the *form*, such as length, width, height or density, are not capable of evoking such feelings. It is only the *essence* that can represent the true power and beauty in every *form*. The *essence* is felt but not seen, for it is from the unseen.

The Secret of Sight

In the year 1812, there lived a famous artist by the name of Emil, who resided in a little cottage in the mountains. The beauties of his surroundings taught him a great deal about the forms of art that exist in nature. Each day he painted what he had learned, and over the years, he produced a large collection of some of the finest paintings on earth. His pictures depicted mountains, trees, birds, animals, plants, rivers, waterfalls, rocks, clouds and everything else that comes from nature's art library. Despite his fame and fortune, Emil was an unhappy man. He could not explain the void in his heart that grew deeper each day even though his paintings excelled in calibre and quality.

He often asked himself, "Each day I produce greater works of art. Why is it then that I do not feel any pride or sense of achievement? Instead, I feel a void in me that grows deeper. I feel less content with my work each day."

Whilst the society placed him on a pedestal and ranked him as one of the greatest artists on earth, poor Emil became ever more frustrated with a burning inner thirst. None of his famous masterpieces could even begin to quench this powerful thirst. One day, as he lay awake in his bed at dawn looking out of the window at the snow-capped mountains, Emil saw a majestic, white dove flying gracefully towards him with the power and speed of an eagle. A few moments later, the bird landed on the window ledge and paused to look at the great artist.

The dove said to Emil, "You are the famous artist that *looks* at everything but *sees* nothing, aren't you?"

Emil, who was most surprised to hear the dove speak, replied, "I beg your pardon, little bird! Of course I do *see* everything around me. Have you not seen my paintings? Have you not recognised the accuracy with which I replicate the mountains, trees, rivers, and snow?"

The dove replied, "My dear Emil, no matter how good you think your art is, the truth is that you *look* but do not *see*."

Offended by this remark, Emil sat up on the bed and snapped, "Throughout my life, if there is one thing that I have done well, it is to paint. I have been able to capture all that I see and produce paintings that are precise. How can you say that an artist like me does not *see*? After all, you are just a little bird that only knows how to fly and sit on trees when you tire!"

The dove looked at Emil with its bright eyes and replied, "Do you know the difference between *looking* and *seeing*?"

Emil angrily replied, "The eyes of an artist must be able to *see* everything, and I mean everything, in order to produce fine paintings."

To that the dove replied, "Indeed Emil, you are so right. An artist must be able to *see* everything in order to produce fine paintings. But you, my dear friend, do not *see*! Hence, you produce paintings that are the best pieces of work that you can generate without *seeing*. Your work is remarkably good for one that only *looks* but does not *see*. But you have a long way to go!"

Emil, who was dejected by this remark, retorted, "If you are such a smart bird, why don't you teach me how to *see*!"

The dove replied, "Firstly, you need to be completely honest with yourself, Emil. You are painfully aware that as you produce greater works of art, there is a void in you that grows bigger each day; and there is a thirst in you that has become unbearable. You are wondering why this is happening to you at a time when you should be celebrating your success. Isn't that true, Emil?"

The dove continued, "You see, Emil, it is because the art you produce continues to excel in only one dimension, which is the dimension of *looking*. However, your work seriously lacks in the dimension of *seeing*, which in fact, is the root cause of your inner void and thirst. In each element of nature lies an *essence* and a *form*. You have tried to master the *form* in your art. Hence, as your replications of the *form* get better, they reveal an obvious absence of the *essence* that gives life and character to the *form*. So far, all you have done is to mechanically copy the things you see. You have not created any art because you have been unable to *see* the *essence* and capture it in your work!"

Emil, who was intrigued by what the dove had said, then asked, "How can I *see* the *essence*? How can I recognise it?"

The dove smiled and replied, "Look at each aspect of nature as if it originates from within you and then radiates outward from you."

The dove continued, "Consider that tall oak tree out there. When you *look* at it, you try to capture the image of the tree as it travels towards your eyes. This is the process of receiving the light that reflects off the tree and comes to your eyes. In this process of receiving lies a total lack of creation. For you to *see* the *essence*, you must create the tree within you and let the light of this creation radiate outward from you until it coincides with the incoming image of the tree you are looking at. Where the two meet is where the *essence* (i.e. radiation) meets the *form* (i.e. reflection). At this point you are truly *seeing* the tree. This is where you can capture its complete image in your painting".

This concept was a little complex for Emil, who, by now had calmed down and had become completely absorbed with what the little bird was saying. He humbly commented, "While I can accept what you are trying to teach me, I cannot say that I fully understand how I can capture the *essence* in my paintings."

The dove replied, "Emil, it is quite simple. Create your paintings by starting with the *essence* within you. If you are trying to paint a bird in the sky, create it within yourself first. Then let the *essence* of that which you have created radiate out from within you to meet the actual *form* of the bird you are looking at. Where the two meet lays the true image that you must capture. When you look at a painting that has been created in this way, it carries a fulfilment that emanates from within the very soul of the artist. If you paint in this manner, you will begin to see real beauty in your work. The more you create in your art, the greater will be the sense of fulfilment that you will enjoy. Where there is fulfilment, there is no void. When you let a pure river of *essence* flow from you, there can be no room for thirst. This, my dear friend, is the answer you have been seeking."

Emil was truly overcome and he said to the dove, "I thank you deeply, from the bottom of my heart, for the pearls of wisdom that you have showered upon me. All my life, I have been blind despite the fact that I have eyes that can *look*.

Today, you have taught me to *see*! For this I will be eternally grateful to you."

The dove replied, "I am glad that you have learned the essential aspect of living, which is the recognition of *essence* and *form*. This, my dear Emil, can be applied to every action and every thought in your life. Remember that you are a focal point of everything that surrounds you. You are like a dot that is surrounded by your entire world, or the universe for that matter. When you look at a dot, it appears small and insignificant in comparison to everything else. To see the dot, your eyes must be outside of the dot. But, imagine for a moment that you could place your eyes inside the dot. What would you see?"

Emil replied, "If my eyes were inside the dot, I would see everything. I mean, I would see the entire universe!"

The dove smiled and said, "That is correct Emil. It all depends on where you place your eyes. If your eyes were outside the dot, all you would see is the tiny *form* of the dot. Yet, once your eyes enter the dot, you can perceive its *essence*, which is indeed infinite, like the universe."

Emil had finally understood *essence*, in a language that appealed to his artistic way of thinking. He remarked, "You are right, it is truly simple. Everything in my world can be perceived from two levels, the *essence* and the *form*. I must learn to appreciate and capture both these aspects in everything that I do. When I go back to the city and see my family and friends, I will now look at them with a different perspective. I used to think my disabled friend Mansour was a cripple because he has no limbs. I considered him to be imperfect. But, how silly of me, I was only looking at his *form*. His *essence* is pure, great and infinite. Now when I meet my friend Mansour, I will see him from a very different perspective too. Now I am ready to learn a great deal from him also."

The dove replied, "You see, my dear Emil, you have finally learnt what so many enlightened souls have preached about. Throughout history, they tried to teach humanity about the *essence* and the *form*. When the great Buddha talked of his enlightenment and taught his followers how to meditate and seek the Light, all he was trying to tell them was to *look* and *see*."

Emil got up from his bed and walked over to the dove, placed the two palms of his hands in humble salutation, and bowed with respect to this enlightened bird. He then asked the dove, "I am now 50 years old. Why did you not visit me sooner with this knowledge?"

The dove smiled and replied, "I have come to you many, many times ever since you were a child. But, each time I came to you, your eyes were shut tight. I whispered in your ear to wake you up, but you never heard me. I felt sad for you because I could feel the void and thirst in you grow each day. Your mind was completely closed, in the midst of your deep sleep, so you could not do anything to help yourself. You are very fortunate that I found you this morning with your eyes open. Look at what you have gained!"

The dove continued, "I visit the homes of so many each day. But, they are all fast asleep, *looking* at everything in their dreams. And, when they awake all they do is to *look* at the world around them. I can only help those who want to help themselves. If they take the trouble to awaken themselves from within they will learn how to *see*. They will then be able to *see* their world and their lives from an infinitely broader perspective. They will be able to rise above their daily problems and issues and gain the power to live an enriched life, with an abundance of everything that they need. They will also be able to recognise the purpose for which they have come into this world. Then, they will be able to use their body and all the other tools that they have been blessed with to fulfil their mission in this life."

Emil then said, "My body is 50 years old. It is aging each day. Have I wasted my gift of having this body by not doing anything about fulfilling my purpose in life?"

The dove smiled and replied, "Emil, no day is ever lost or wasted. You have indeed achieved a part of your life's mission so far. You have gained knowledge from your daily experiences. You have inspired others with your paintings. You have brought joy into the lives of many. Today is a special day in your life, because you have learned about *essence* and *form*. *Form* is limited in time and space. *Essence* is timeless and unlimited. Think each day about these important matters and you will gain the ability to perceive everything from an infinitely broader perspective. This will be an excellent start..."

THE PULSE OF LIFE

When we look at our fellow human beings or other living creatures, we ask ourselves, "Where does their essence reside?" The answer is simple. The essence is unseen and has no dimensions. Therefore, it cannot be confined within in any physical space that is enveloped by three dimensions. The essence exists in every atom and every cell of every living thing. Let us reflect once again on the example of the dying patient, Charles:

At 10:59 p.m., Charles is lying on a bed in the intensive care unit of the hospital. He has suffered a severe heart attack and the doctors are trying to do everything they can to save him. At 10:59 p.m., his heart is beating and his brain and body are functioning. Then, something happens. One minute later, at 11 p.m., Charles is pronounced dead. A few minutes later, the doctors and nurses leave the intensive care room, after covering his face with a white sheet. In a day or two, Charles will be buried or cremated and he will be seen no more. In terms of form, Charles's form will have come to its end. The question is, "What did Charles have at 10:59 p.m. that he did not have at 11 p.m.? What did he lose in that one minute that took him from being alive to being pronounced dead?" The answer is essence, which some may call soul, spirit or life energy. When Charles was alive, we could all see and feel him. His essence gave expression to his form. Now that the essence is gone, Charles, the form, is no more.

One night when Charles was a younger man, he was playing with his son Samuel, whilst putting him to bed. As Charles tucked him in, Samuel said, "I love you dad."

Charles replied with a question, "What is it about me that you love, Samuel?"

Samuel pointed at Charles's chest and said, "You."
To that, Charles replied, "That is not me, that is my chest! Tell me, Samuel, what is it about me that you love?"

The only word the little boy could say was "you", because each time he tried to point at what he thought "you" was, he was unable to express himself.

Between 10:59 p.m. and 11 p.m., it was the "you," the *essence* that had left. Now, Samuel had no father. The *form*, or body was dead and all Samuel could do was to bury or cremate it. What was it that he was burying or cremating? Was it Charles? Was it the father he loved? If the *form* represented everything that Charles was, then how could Samuel bury or burn this *form* that he loved so much? The truth is that the "you", which the poor little boy had tried so hard to point at, was the *essence* that had left the *form*. Every memory of his father rested in the "you" and not in the object he had buried or cremated. Hence, *essence* is what invokes feelings of love in us. *Essence* is what gives character to everything. *Essence* is what represents life in everything. *Essence* is everything!

In our daily lives we should try to learn to recognise *essence* in everything around us. *Essence* is the common element that binds humanity together. It is the common thread that makes us one with our friends, loved ones, neighbours, and every living creature on this planet and beyond. Recognising the *essence* helps us to integrate the similarities that exist between ourselves, rather than to expand on our differences.

When we look at a painting of a beautiful landscape, we admire the colours that we see – the greens, blues, yellows and all other shades. Whilst each colour is an essential aspect of the painting, every colour gets its definition from the white background on which the painting was created. Without this white background, the blue would not be blue and green would not be green. Blue is blue because white exists. Green is green because white exists. The *essence* of the painting is indeed its white background. A similar parallel can be drawn when we look at *essence* in humanity. We are all woven together as one through *essence*. Yet we are all different in our own ways, like every colour is in the painting. Therefore, recognising and understanding *form* and *essence* is essential in developing our outlook towards life. If we truly understand both these aspects, we can come closer to achieving *zero conflict*. We can learn to appreciate, understand and admire our differences, while recognising the common bond that exists between us all through *essence*. Only seeing our differences pulls us apart. If we focus solely on our differences, we move away from one another, in every way. Yet, if we can identify and recognise our differences as emanating from a common *essence*, then every difference in itself becomes an aspect, which can be integrated to give us a holistic view and understanding of our fellow beings and everything around us. *Essence* unites and integrates differences to yield strength from our diversities. This, in fact, is the genesis of the phrase *Diversity is Strength*.

Recognising the existence of *essence* and *form* brings a healthy, positive and flexible outlook towards life. If we can see that a greater reality exists within every *form*, then we may be able to experience beauty in all that we encounter. If we can realise that humanity is woven together as one through *essence*, then we would become more understanding and forgiving towards one another. No human being or creature is "bad". We all have an *essence* that is pure, innocent and beautiful. What differentiates us at a material level, apart from our physical *forms*, is the actions and perceptions of our minds. Even when we look at people who hurt us or hurt others, we should always be able to recognise that their actions are driven by their minds. Their *essence* can be nothing but pure, like the white background of the painting. If we can appreciate this fundamental principle, then we will be able to avoid conflict in our lives, because we will be viewing everything that happens within and around us from an infinitely broader perspective. This is an essential step in our journey *towards zero conflict*.

Seeds of Resolution

❋ In order to learn to recognise the *essence* in every *form*, we need to take a few moments each day to reflect on our own *essence*. We need to recognise that we are all part of a great picture, which includes us and everything that surrounds us. We are all part of a common Source or Origin. Every living thing has its roots in this common Origin. This recognition is one of *unity*, which grows within us as we meditate on the words:

"I AM EVERYTHING AND EVERYTHING IS ME."

❋ As we repeat this simple phrase, with our mind fully focused on its *essence*, we will learn to bond with our loved ones, families, friends, neighbours, humanity at large, and our environment. These words will help to strengthen the common roots that we all share with one another through our Origin.

My Reflections

Now   date: / /   .

My Reflections

One Year Hence   date: / /   .

My Reflections

Chapter 3

HARNESSING THE PRESENT

"Life is a series of crossroads..."

One Saturday evening, I sat in front of the ocean on the rocks of Puerto de la Cruz, Tenerife, and looked out in awe at the magnificent sunset. The ocean had taken on a beautiful crimson colour, reflecting multiple shades of red, pink and orange in the sky. It was truly a precious moment. I looked at the horizon where the sky met the ocean and thought to myself, "Isn't it wonderful to be alive?"

I then began to think about being alive. I asked myself, "When am I truly alive?" As I reflected upon this question, I cast my mind back at the past, which seemed very long indeed. In fact, the past, or history, is infinite. I turned my thoughts towards the future and realised that it too was very long. Indeed, the future is also infinite. Then, I recognised that there is a very fine line that separates the past from the future. This fine line is the present, which is extremely short in duration. Yet, the only time that I am truly alive is in the present. The past is a memory and the future is an expectation. The only reality that exists is the present, which is truly the most important moment in my life. The present is filled with wonderful powers for it is the only moment at which I can do anything to influence my life, my future and my destiny.

Life is a series of crossroads. At each crossroad, we have a choice to make. We can turn left at the crossroad, which will lead us to a new set of crossroads, or we can turn right and be led towards a different set of crossroads. We can also go straight and end up at yet another set of crossroads. We cannot go back, for that is not possible. The choices that we make at each crossroad lead us to the next set of crossroads. This journey from crossroad to crossroad is called destiny. Each choice that we make at a crossroad shapes our destiny. It is noteworthy that the only time at which we can actually make a choice is in the present, or now. Therefore, if we truly harness the present, we can govern the future in a positive manner, and hence, our destiny.

Take a simple example of young Simon drinking a glass of water. He fills the glass, brings it to his lips and drinks the water. Once the water has been drunk, the past will have recorded this event by stating that, "Simon filled the glass, brought it to his lips and drank the water."

Let us examine this event as it interacts between the past and the future. When Simon originally lifted the glass to fill it, the future would have said, "Water will enter the glass." Once the glass was full, the past would have recorded the full glass. At that point, the future would have said, "The glass will reach Simon's lips." Once this had happened, history would have recorded that "The glass had reached his lips." At this point, the future would have said, "The water will be drunk," and when this had occurred, history would have recorded the fact accordingly.

Isn't it interesting how the past and future almost flow into each other? Yet, there is a very fine line that separates the past and the future, which is the present or now. How long is the present? One could argue that it is a day long, or an hour long, or a second long or a microsecond long. Or does it almost not exist? It is clear that the present is considerably shorter than the *past or the future. Yet it is the present that causes the past to record an event, and it is the present that dictates the direction that the future will take.*

Let us consider Simon's glass of water once more. At the beginning of the event, the future would have said, "The glass will be filled." *Once full, it would have become an event of the past. Then, the future would have said,* "Simon will bring the glass to his lips in order to drink the water." *But, if at that present moment, Simon chose to pour the water out of the glass rather than bring it to his lips, then he would have changed the future! The future would now say,* "Simon will put the glass back on the shelf rather than bring it to his lips!" *In this small example, we can see how the present, short as it may be, totally dictates the past and the future.*

Therefore, it is very important for us to learn to respect the present, for that is one of the most important aspects of living. The present governs everything. Some people lose the present because they are so worried about the future. They need to realise that the present actually governs the future! Others lose the present because they live in the memories of the past. They must realise that the past is purely a product of what the present was at some given point in time. Therefore, our aim must be to live in the present fully and correctly. We should utilise every bit of the present wisely to help us achieve our life's purpose.

As we seek to achieve zero conflict *in our lives, we need to fully understand the importance of living in the present. Both the past and the future embody sources of conflict, which may take the form of worries, concerns, anxiety, bitterness, disappointment, anger and many other emotions. Yet, in the present, there exists neutrality, empowered with pure energy, within which we can make our decisions and enjoy the moments when we are truly alive. It is only in the present that we can eliminate the conflicts that reside within and around us. It is only in the present that we can truly exercise all the principles that are set forth in this book, which will help us to progress towards a life of zero conflict. It is only in the present that we can fully explore, realise, embrace and utilise the pure energy that we are!*

CARVING DESTINY

Michael was born and raised in a small village in northern England, called Chatton. He grew up as an average child, making choices at every crossroad in his life. His choices ranged from little decisions, such as what toys he should play with, to the bigger ones, such as whether he should spend his summer holidays with his mother or his father, who were divorced.

The story of Michael's destiny begins at a crossroad, when he was 22 years old. He had just completed a degree in electrical engineering at Newcastle University. He was in love with Alice, a girl from an aristocratic English family, who was also graduating from the same university with a degree in international politics. After their graduation ceremony, Alice posed the all-important question to Michael about marriage and their future together. This was a critical crossroad for both of them. Their choices would govern the direction that their lives would take thereafter.

Michael decided that he was not ready for marriage because he wanted to travel the world and gain experience in his career before settling down. Alice was not willing to wait for him. A painful parting followed that took each of them towards their own destinies. Michael accepted a job offer with a consulting engineering company in Hong Kong. Two years later, he married a Chinese girl, by the name of Cathy, who came from a devout Christian family. The initial years of their marriage were very happy, and Cathy made every effort to ensure that Michael went to church every Sunday. This was something that he had never done before because he was not a religious person. They had two daughters and a son, and their lives were shaping up beautifully, as one happy family. As Michael's interest in religion grew, out of curiosity, he began to study the Asian religions. He found himself being drawn towards Buddhism and its principles. Two years later, he converted from Christianity to Buddhism, much to the dismay of Cathy. Michael began to spend a great deal of time at the temple and five years later, he announced to Cathy that he was leaving her and the children in order to become a monk at a holy temple in Tibet. Neither Cathy nor the children could do anything to change his mind.

Michael settled in very well with his new Tibetan way of life. Over the years, he rose in rank to become the Head Monk at the temple. He was very happy with all that he had accomplished there. Several years later, Tibet was attacked by the Chinese, who arrested all the leaders of the Buddhist temples. Michael found himself in a prison, in the northern mountain ranges of China, cold, hungry, and feeling very bitter. He spent the rest of his life in prison and died alone. He was buried in an unmarked grave.

This was the ultimate destiny that he had achieved. Was Michael's life a success or a failure, we may ask? We will never know the answer to this question, because we do not know the purpose for which Michael had come into this world. We do not know anything about the mission of his life. If we were to attempt to judge his successes and failures, we would need to be very careful in reflecting upon the standards by which we choose to assess Michael's success and failure. If we did so, we would soon come to the conclusion that, in fact, we are not in a position to judge anyone or anything. What we do know, however, is that Michael exercised choice at every crossroad, leading to his death in a Chinese prison.

Let us examine some of the crossroads in Michael's life. We can do this by asking the following questions:

What if he had married Alice?
What if Cathy had not pushed him towards religion?
What if he had not converted to Buddhism?
What if he had listened to Cathy and not gone to Tibet?
What if he had not accepted the role of Head Monk?
What if? What if? What if?

Each of the above questions represents an important crossroad in Michael's life. If he had made a different choice at any one of the crossroads, his ultimate destiny may have been very different. The same is true for all of us, when we reflect upon our lives. Let us go back to Michael's first crossroad at the age of 22, when Alice asked him to marry her. Let us now look at a new scenario, where Michael had made a different decision at that crossroad.

43

Michael agreed to marry Alice. He joined a British engineering firm in London and Alice worked for the British Government's Ministry of Foreign Affairs. They bought a beautiful home in Kent and lived a very happy life together. Both were driven by their careers and hence, having children was not on the agenda for the first fifteen years of their marriage. During this time, Alice aged rapidly and her health was always poor. Then, they had a son whom they named Stuart. He was born prematurely and remained unhealthy throughout his childhood. Alice gave up her job for a little while to look after Stuart. Michael worked on the development of new technologies in the medical industry, successfully applying his knowledge of electronics and electrical engineering. When Michael received a job offer from a leading research company based in Boston in the United States, he moved there with Alice and Stuart. He was very successful at what he did and over the next ten years his inventions revolutionised certain important aspects of medical science. He also became a multi-millionaire. Alice became a professor at Harvard University, where she rose to the rank of Dean of her faculty. Michael and Alice were so immersed in their work that they scarcely spent time with Stuart, who had grown up into a shy and lonely young man. Stuart chose to practice homosexuality. His parents were completely unaware of their son's life. One day, Michael and Alice learned that Stuart had contracted AIDS and that the chances of his survival were virtually nil. This news was absolutely devastating for them. Remorseful and broken hearted, they repeatedly asked themselves where they had gone wrong. Of course, there were many painful answers to that question. Michael's world came to a complete halt. He gave up his profession to spend time with Stuart during his final nine months. Medical science could not do anything to save his beloved son's life. Stuart passed away peacefully one afternoon, in the arms of his mother. Alice sank into a deep depression, from which she never recovered. After Stuart's death, Michael decided to dedicate his wealth and skills in pursuit of solutions to assist people with AIDS worldwide. Michael helped save the lives of hundreds of thousands of people. His efforts won him much recognition around the word, including the Nobel Prize. He died at the age of 62. His funeral was attended by the heads of state of many nations. The world mourned his passing. The newspapers, radio and television networks celebrated his life in more languages than he could ever have imagined.

We may ask the question, "Was Michael's life a success?" Once again, we will never know the answer to this question, because we will never know what the mission of his life really was. However, we can see that the one choice that he made at the age of 22, regarding marriage to Alice, led him to a completely different destiny and ending.

Imagine the lonely death in a Chinese prison in comparison to the celebration of his life throughout the world as a man who helped save thousands of lives. Imagine the pain of losing his son versus voluntarily leaving his family to go to Tibet. We can also ask numerous questions about the other crossroads in his life with Alice, such as:

What if Alice and he had not been so engrossed in their careers?
What if they had started a family sooner?
What if Michael had not taken up the job offer in the USA?
What if he had spent more time with Stuart, helping and guiding him?

*What if he had continued with his work and business after
Stuart's death, rather than embarking on the crusade
against AIDS?*
What if? What if? What if?

It is easy to see how a different choice exercised by Michael
at each crossroad could have led him in a completely different
direction. The same is true for each one of us. Every decision we
take at every crossroad governs the course of our destiny. If we
think of all the combinations that are possible, with respect to
the impact of our choices, we begin to realise that life is not as
simple as we often treat it to be. It is not something that we can
afford to waste. It is a precious gift that we must appreciate and
harness, for every second that we are alive represents a
crossroad. Therefore, we should aim to make wise decisions that
are not clouded by elements of conflict and other non-
productive aspects of our intellectual make-up. If we seek to
draw inspirations from our *essence*, which embodies the pure
energy and wisdom that resides within us, then we will be able
to make wise decisions that will lead us towards the true ending
that we had sought to achieve at birth. A life that is led by
decisions drawn from inner wisdom is not an ordinary destiny. It
is an *exalted destiny*. The most important point to recognise is
that each and every choice that we make at our crossroads can
only be made in the present. It is only in the present that we can
fully explore, realise, embrace and utilise our true potential. It is
only in the present that we can chart the course of the future.

It is no coincidence that when we write *now* backwards, it
reads, *won*. The key to success, happiness and fulfilment is to
harness *now*, for then, every moment of our lives will have been
won!

Seeds of Resolution

❀ In order to reaffirm the importance of the present moment, we should pause for a few moments in the midst of our busy schedules, close our eyes, and repeat the phrase:

"Now is Real"

❀ These words carry a special energy that reaffirms within us the importance of the present moment.

❀ Repeating these words when we find ourselves preoccupied and worried about events to come, will help bring us back to the present, where we can act decisively towards implementing solutions to our problems.

❀ When we find ourselves engrossed in thoughts of the past, these words will help us to recognise that we are losing our precious moments of empowerment, which can only be found in the present.

My Reflections

Now   date: / / .

My Reflections

One Year Hence   date: / / .

My Reflections

Chapter 4

THE POWER OF FLOW

Rigidity versus Flexibility

When one looks at different forms, one can recognise the difference between the rigid ones and the flexible ones. Rigidity and flexibility represent the fundamental characteristics of form. For instance, a glass of water represents pure flexibility (water) embodied in pure rigidity (glass). If you drop the glass, it shatters into a hundred fragments because glass is very rigid. The shattered fragments are equally rigid. Yet, as the glass shatters, the water simply flows out of it and gently spreads out on the floor. The rigid breaks up upon impact, beyond repair. The flexible simply flows out of the very same situation.

When we look at our lives, we need to carefully scrutinise our areas of rigidity and flexibility. I went to a boarding school in England where we had a Matron who was responsible for taking care of us in the boarding house. For Matron, each minute and hour of the day was completely organised with painful precision. Everything she did was perfectly set within a tight and rigid framework. I rarely saw Matron smile. If any of us did the slightest thing to disrupt her carefully organised activities, we would be in for a major telling-off, and the rest of the day would pass with her being in a foul mood! Such was the life of our dear Matron. I cannot ever remember seeing her relaxed, being light hearted, or bursting out with laughter. She was usually angry, uptight or in tears, no matter where she went. She was a good example of rigidity in life. I would not be surprised if she suffered from ulcers or heart trouble as she aged.

To date, I have come across many people like Matron. Some show their rigidity in a very obvious manner. Others are subtler. As soon as their rigidity is put to the test, they shatter like glass, causing immense pain to themselves and to all those around them. Imagine the pressure that goes with such conformity! Such pressure triggers unhealthy stress, which in turn triggers physical and mental health problems.

One day as I took a walk along a construction site of a skyscraper in downtown Toronto, I saw workers trying to erect a tall pillar. They used cables to get the pillar to stand. The pillar was completely rigid. The flexibility of the cables was essential to get such a rigid structure to stand upright. I remembered Matron. Her life would have been so much better had she been supported by such flexibility. But, she would not allow it because flexibility enables movement or change, which to Matron was a disruption to her ways. I observed that the construction workers pulled back at the cables in varying directions, causing the pillar to move until it found its final place of rest. I thought to myself, "What if this pillar were twice as tall?" One would not have to be a genius to realise that the taller this rigid structure grew, the more easily it could crack and crumble. Even the tallest skyscrapers in the world are built with flexible structures within their core to prevent them from falling apart during earthquakes, high winds and storms. All rigid structures need flexible aspects within them to help them survive. The same is true for people. We all need room to move from within if we are to survive. I wish I knew then what I know now. I would surely have tried to help Matron, even at the risk of being expelled!

THE FLOWING RIVER

*C*onflict arises very easily where there is rigidity. Life has one constant feature — *change*. *Rigidity* is challenged by *change*, causing immense conflict. *Flexibility* embraces and accommodates *change*, thus reducing *conflict*. Ultimate *flexibility* is expressed in water. If a human being were to be as *flexible* as water, he or she would come very close to *zero conflict*. Water flows with speed. Water turns with ease. Water takes the shape of its container. Water carries powerful energies within itself. Water stores salts, minerals and nutrients, within its molecular structure. Water expands and contracts. It changes forms from solid to liquid to vapour. Water heals. Water cleanses. Water brings life. Such are the attributes of ultimate *flexibility*.

While we can all live our lives with varying degrees of self-organisation and discipline, our inner feelings and how we perceive the world around us should be based on pure *flexibility*, like water. We should aim to fit into our circumstances like water fits into its container. We should flow through life like water. We should expand and contract from within to accommodate our stresses and strains. We should heal and cleanse ourselves, our fellow beings and our environment like water heals and cleanses.

Of course, this way of thinking can not manifest within us overnight. Like the pillar at the construction site, we should allow flexible cables to assist us. To start with, we might allow those around us who do not conform to our ways, to help us see that there are other ways of doing the same thing. When we find ourselves getting very angry and stressed because our ways are not being followed, we should stop and think of a flowing river and imagine its crystal clear water gently flowing over the rocks. This vision will teach us to flow over the issues that are causing us stress and frustration. We should ask ourselves, "Does this really matter?" Frequently, the answer to this question will be, "no". We should place our challenges in their correct perspective by saying to ourselves, "I will flow into this situation and I will flow out of it. *I am free and I can flow.* Nothing can bind me or hold me down, for I am the *river.*" As we think about the *river,* we will start to feel like a *river.* We will begin to embrace the power of its *flexibility.*

THE POWER OF PURE POTENTIAL

Each one of us possesses a pure and infinite *potential* that empowers us to achieve whatever it is that we strive for. Consider an 18-year-old boy, by the name of Tony, who picks up a snowball at the bottom of a mountain and carries it all the way to the peak, in a small plastic bag. With each step of his ascension up the mountain, the snowball gains potential energy, which reaches its maximum level at the peak. The snowball now represents Tony's pure *potential.* It is bursting with energy and desire to roll downhill, and to create a whole host of events along its journey. Tony then unleashes his *potential* by letting go of the little snowball. He watches it roll downhill as it grows into a huge, white ball of ice. He then follows the snowball in his sledge until it finally comes to rest in the valley. He looks at the huge boulder of ice that has been created, from what was once a little snowball. He reflects on the moment when he stood at the top of the mountain. *What did he have then?* Was the snowball a huge boulder of ice at that point? If not, what was it? What Tony possessed at the top of the mountain was a powerful, unseen *potential*, which had grown stronger with each step that he had taken as he climbed up the mountain. At the peak, this *potential* was at its maximum. It had the power to give birth to a huge boulder of ice. All Tony had to do was to let this *potential* express itself by letting the little snowball go! Such is the truth about the pure *potential* that we all possess. We are limitless and can achieve whatever goals we set for ourselves.

Another example is that of a *river*, which starts its journey from the top of a mountain. Like the snowball, it too contains pure *potential*, which yields flow. Yet, flow can only come from *flexibility*. As the *river* flows downhill, it does so with a natural ease, energy and grace that is synonymous with true *accomplishment*. Therefore, it takes *flexibility* to realise our true *potential* and to achieve *accomplishment*.

When water flows, it becomes pure. A *river* needs to flow in order to maintain its purity. When we build a dam in the midst of a flowing *river*, we kill its flow. After all, a dam is simply a *rigid* wall that destroys flow. The water behind a dam stagnates, dies and begins to smell foul. In the same way, in our lives, we should allow our *potential* to express itself through flow. We should avoid being *rigid* and building dams that kill our flow. We should also avoid imposing our *rigidity* upon others by building dams in their lives, which ultimately stifle them and destroy their flow. Building dams is a sure way of giving birth to *conflict* and fuelling its flames. This is true for all levels of relationships, from our own inner selves, to our spouses, families, friends, loved ones, colleagues and acquaintances. When we find ourselves suffering from *conflicts* in our relationships, we need to ask ourselves some important questions, such as, "Am I being *rigid?* Am I building dams? Do I need to be more *flexible?* Am I flowing freely?" After some reflection, the answers will usually be quite obvious!

FLOWING UPHILL

An important point to remember is that water does not flow *uphill.* If we find ourselves struggling very hard with a situation, then we may be trying to flow *uphill.* This is a signal to stop and review the situation, and to ask ourselves if there is a better way of dealing with the situation at hand. Can we flow around the situation like the *river?* More often than not, there are easier ways of dealing with difficult situations. We need to be aware that we are trying to flow *uphill* and this will automatically cause us to seek better alternatives. We should recognise that we possess pure *potential* and that we must always aim to flow *downhill* in order to achieve true *accomplishment,* as illustrated by the experience of Tony's little snowball.

A few years ago, my wife and I took a Swissair flight from Madrid to Zurich, en route to Johannesburg. After we had boarded the aircraft at Madrid airport, we were told that the ramp of the catering truck was stuck under the rear door of the aircraft. All the passengers were asked to disembark so that the plane could rise by an inch or two as a result of the reduction in its weight. The flight engineers hoped that this would help free the ramp of the catering truck from the rear door. Upon disembarking the plane, I walked over to the catering truck, curious to see how they would dislodge the ramp without damaging the aircraft. The engineers struggled frantically without any success. There was great commotion! Then they started to offload the baggage from the aircraft, with the hope that this would further reduce the weight of the aircraft. Just then I remembered the *river* flowing *uphill!* I said to myself, "There must be a better way of solving this problem." My eyes wandered from the stuck ramp to the tires of the truck. There was the answer. Deflate the tires by 50 percent and the ramp would dislodge itself automatically! All the commotion would not then be necessary. The *river* would flow *downhill* freely! I suggested this solution to the engineers and the problem was promptly solved. Therefore, there are always alternative ways to solve problems. When we try to flow *uphill*, we burn up energy and encounter pain, anger and frustration. These are primary sources of *conflict.* Yet a simple change in approach can solve the problem, with no conflict. All we have to remember is that the *river* must flow with least resistance. We should try to avoid *uphill* flows!

THE WATERFALL

When we find ourselves facing a catastrophe that causes us deep hurt, we must remember the *waterfall*, where the river flows over the rocks with great energy, in the midst of much turmoil. At the bottom of the *waterfall* the waters are calm again. This is so for each and every one of us because life always brings challenging situations in order for us to gain experience and knowledge. When we find ourselves in difficulty, one option is to say to ourselves, "This is not permanent. I am in the *waterfall*. I have power. I am flowing to calmer waters."

Remember, if we think that our situation is unbearable, then we should be aware that there are others who are facing much worse conditions than we are. Consider the following four scenarios:

It is 12 noon in New York. Marie Claire is sitting in a beautician's chair. She has come to have a pimple on her face removed. She looks at the pimple in the mirror and bursts into tears. She says, "This is horrible. It looks so ugly. I hate it!"

The beautician tries to console Marie Claire and says, "Relax, my dear, we will soon get rid of it."

At the same hour, in Seattle, Caroline receives an urgent call at the office from her neighbour. Her house is on fire! She rushes home to be greeted by the ruins and ashes, which only a few hours ago was her home. All her possessions have been burned beyond recognition. She does not have any insurance coverage because, as a single mother, she can barely get by on her salary. Unlike Marie Claire's beautician, there is no one there to tell Caroline, "Relax, my dear, we will take care of it!"

Further south, in Los Angeles, Michael has had a motorcycle accident and the paramedics are trying desperately to save his crushed leg. All their attempts fail and Michael's leg has to be amputated back at the hospital. When Michael awakens, he is told that he has lost his leg, and he bursts into tears. Because his leg is gone, the surgeon cannot say to him, "Relax, my dear, we will take care of it!"

At the same time in Central Africa, there is a small village hospital that is full to capacity with people infected with the deadly *Ebola* virus. Jonathan's family — his wife, two daughters and son lie curled up with pain, in a small, dark room. Jonathan looks helplessly at his loved ones as each one of them dies before his eyes. With deep grief in his heart, he awaits his turn to depart from this world. There is no one with him who can say, "Relax, my dear, we will take care of it."

At any given moment, people in different places are going through such different experiences. The question is, would Marie Claire, sitting in the beautician's chair, be willing to trade places with Caroline, who has lost all her worldly possessions? Is Marie Claire's problem really that bad in comparison? Alternatively, would Caroline be willing to trade places with Michael, who has just lost his leg? Would Michael be willing to swap places with Jonathan, who has witnessed the death of his entire family before his very own eyes? These questions teach us a very important lesson on how people perceive their problems. Each one of these characters feels that his or her world has come to an end. They believe that they are correct about the way they feel. If each one of them were able to view their problem from a broader perspective, they would be able to deal with their situations in a less hurtful manner, perhaps with the exception of Jonathan. We all live in our own little worlds, where we tend to be completely engrossed with our problems and challenges. We are usually oblivious to the difficulties that are being faced by others. We can create enormous internal and external *conflicts* as a result of the selfish manner in which we perceive and manage our problems.

In the midst of our crises, we should remember that we are in the *waterfall*. We need to believe in ourselves and in the calmer waters that lie ahead. We need to be appreciative of the larger *waterfalls* around us, through which our fellow beings are trying to navigate their way. After all, our own *waterfall* may only be a little dewdrop compared to what others may be facing. We may be like Marie Claire with the pimple, creating within ourselves the same level of anguish and panic as poor Jonathan, watching his dying family. If we are able to capture this trend of thought and put into practice this important aspect of living, then we will find ourselves celebrating our good fortune, in the midst of our crises. We will be able to treat our challenges and tribulations as *speed bumps* rather than *head-on collisions!* In the absence of our self-created anguish, we may be able to see our way clearly through every storm in our lives, and hence creatively seek permanent solutions to our problems. This is an important key in minimizing conflicts in our lives.

THE WISDOM OF ALICE

A problem can be as big as we make it or it can be as small as we want it to be. Sharing Michael's hospital ward is Alice, a 40-year-old mother of two children, who has lost both her legs due to a serious polio infection. Alice moves around the hospital in her wheelchair, smiling and chatting with patients and their visitors. She is delighted each evening to see her little ones when they came to visit her. She laughs and smiles all the time. She finds great joy in smelling the yellow roses that her husband Richard brings for her every day. Michael looks at her and says, "Alice, how can you be so happy? You have no limbs."

Alice replies, "I am alive, aren't I? I have two hands, don't I? I can move around with my hands, can't I? I have lots to be grateful for! Look at my children. Aren't they lovely? Aren't they precious? They give me so much joy when I play with them. Look at my husband Richard, he loves me so much. Look at these beautiful flowers he has brought for me. Aren't they priceless? Can you not see his love radiating out of every petal of that yellow rose? How can I *not* be happy?"

In the midst of our crises, we should remember and reflect on Alice's words. She is a living *river!* She flows with joy through her difficult circumstances. Indeed, the banks of her *river* have shrunk. But downstream, they expand once again. So she shrinks and expands as she flows, and in doing so, she feels no pain, no anger and no frustration. Alice lives her life like a *river* that is heading to the *ocean*. She is flowing freely to her *Source*. She looks forward to every moment that lies ahead of her. Wouldn't it be interesting for Marie Claire to meet Alice? Perhaps her pimple would take on a whole new meaning!

Seeds of Resolution

Embracing the Lake

* At the end of a tiring, hectic, pressure-filled day, try sitting back comfortably and focusing your thoughts on a *lake*.

* Like the *river*, you have flowed through the day, but now it is time to stand still.

* Imagine a beautiful *lake*, whose water glitters in the early morning sunshine.

* Imagine that you are looking at yourself in this *lake*. The water is so still that you can clearly see your face in it.

* The stillness of the *lake* has made the water become a mirror for you.

* This is where you can find great peace.

* Think of the stillness and calmness and allow yourself to drift into this stillness.

* Remember that water is like an elusive mirror.

* When it flows in the *river*, in the midst of its turbulence, you cannot see your face in it.

* But when it stands still in the *lake*, you can discover yourself in it!

* So, each day, spend a few minutes being like the lake and cherish the peace that comes to you from its stillness.

My Reflections

Now

date: / / .

64

My Reflections

One Year Hence   date: / / .

My Reflections

Chapter 5

THE NEUTRAL ZONE

Polarity

Polarity *is a word that we have all encountered at one time or another, especially during our schooling days. For example, the earth has* polarity, *which rests in its north and south apexes. We call them the North and South Poles. Magnets have* polarity, *where like poles repel and unlike poles attract. Electrical currents have negative and positive charges. Mathematics has plus and minus signs. Our daily decisions have pros and cons. Every argument has at least two sides. These are some examples of* polarity, *which illustrate the extremities within which it exists.*

While polarity *itself is an important aspect of every situation, it can also be a significant source of* conflict *if we dwell totally within it. People who always consider the negative aspects of everything can be defined as being* "negatively polarised". *Such people tend to be suspicious and pessimistic by nature. Their* polarity *is reflected in their words and actions, which can ultimately become sources of their inner and outer* conflicts.

By contrast, there are people who only consider the positive aspects of every situation. Such people tend to be optimistic and sometimes naïve about the realities of their lives. Such people can be defined as being "positively polarised". *While* negative polarisation *can create greater conflicts compared to* positive polarisation, *it is important to recognise the fact that* polarity *causes* conflict. *Therefore, the answer to overcoming conflict lies in seeking equilibrium in everything. This is where the* "neutral zone" *lies.*

The following story of two Martian students illustrates how we can begin to discover the neutral zone...

THE MARTIAN PROJECT

In the year 2077, Ozzy, an undergraduate Martian, receives a mandate from his university to study the *perceptions* of human beings living on planet earth. Instead of conducting his study by simulating human beings in a local Martian zoo, Ozzy opts to come to earth so that he can come in touch with the real thing. The travel expense is nominal as Interplanetary Safaris is running a special promotion, where Martians are encouraged to come to earth and learn about human beings in their real habitat. His research partner, Commie, joins Ozzy. A day after their arrival on this new, intriguing planet, young Ozzy and Commie find themselves in downtown Manhattan, amidst busy streets swarming with cabs and hoards of people rushing in different directions. Ozzy has brought with him a special device called a "perceptometer," which allows him to shrink in size, lodge himself in a human brain and record all its *perceptions.* Commie has brought with him an equally advanced device called the "factometer," which is capable of recording the underlying *reality* in every event. So, while Ozzy's perceptometer records *perceptions,* Commie's factometer provides the facts, or *"reality check".* The combination of these two instruments provides the basis for an excellent experiment that tests *perceptions* versus *reality.* Of course, they now had to find an appropriate human subject, whose brain could play host to Ozzy for a few hours.

As Commie and Ozzy search around Manhattan, they see Frankie, a tall man with frizzy blond hair, frantically cleaning the windshield of a car that has stopped at a set of traffic lights. The quick-thinking Ozzy says to Commie, "That's our man. He is perfect! He gets to look into every car that stops at the traffic lights while cleaning its windshield. He quickly develops a perception of what is going on in the car, even though he doesn't have a clue about what is really happening. Then, after he has cleaned the windshield, he shouts and screams for money. He dances about like a clown when he receives a good tip and utters profanity when he feels short-changed. He is definitely our man."

In a flash, Ozzy and Commie start setting up their equipment. Commie finds a convenient spot on top of the traffic light, where he quickly conducts the final calibrations on his factometer. Simultaneously, Ozzy makes his way into Frankie's brain, where he wires his perceptometer. When all systems have been set up, Ozzy and Commie are able to communicate instantaneously, on a second-by-second basis.

Just then, a black Mercedes Benz 990 stops at the traffic light. This is one of the finest luxury vehicles in the world, whose price tag is equivalent to twenty years of Frankie's earnings. Frankie proceeds to clean its windshield. As he looks inside the car, he sees an obese, bald man in the driver's seat with a grim face and sweaty forehead. Sitting next to him is a beautiful young lady, with tears in her eyes, looking very sad and depressed. Frankie says to himself, "What a horrible, fat, rich man! Look at what he has done to this beautiful young lady. He must have physically abused her, or tormented her emotionally, or done something worse. He looks like a pervert! Such fat, rich, ugly people should be shot, with no questions asked!"

The lights turn green and the driver of the Mercedes gives Frankie a five-dollar bill and drives off. Frankie yells out, "Yeah, yeah, rich man. Go buy the world!"

Ozzy's perceptometer records this entire event, as perceived by Frankie. This *perception* is relayed to Commie, who shakes his head with disbelief as he checks the data on his factometer. His system, which is the *reality check* for the situation, shows the vehicle belonging to Sir Sigmund Bailey, a famous philanthropist who built schools, hospitals and shelters for poor people all over the world. Some twelve hours earlier, there had been a plane crash outside Atlantic City, which had claimed the life of Sir Bailey. His body was now being flown to New York's La Guardia airport, as part of the funeral arrangements. The driver of the car was Mikhail, a distant cousin of Sigmund and an auto mechanic by trade. Mikhail was a simple man with little or no personal wealth. The lady sitting next to him was Maggie, the eldest daughter of Sir Bailey. Mikhail and Maggie were on their way to La Guardia airport to receive the body of their beloved Sigmund!

Commie looks at Frankie and says to himself, "This subject has serious *negative polarisation.*"

Just then, Frankie walks over to another car that has stopped at the traffic lights. It is an old, white, Pontiac Polaris, one of the smallest and cheapest cars available. In it there are two women and a child. The driver is a well-built, masculine looking 55-year-old woman. Next to her is a younger woman, who is slim and beautiful, like one of the models that Frankie had seen in a ripped-out page of an old *Vogue* magazine. "Boy is she ever beautiful," Frankie says to himself. He stares at her as he cleans the windshield, and wonders if the two women are lesbians.

Why else would an older masculine-looking woman be with such a feminine supermodel? As his eyes drift towards the back seat, he sees a little 2-year-old girl, strapped in a child seat, bawling her eyes out. The child looks terribly distressed and yet, the two women seem perfectly content ignoring her. "What kind of women are they?" he says aloud. With exasperation in his face, he continues, "There is a little kid crying her eyes out in the back seat and they don't even seem to care! How can they be so oblivious and how can they continue to smile and behave as if nothing were happening? Could they have kidnapped the child? Could they be a part of a child slavery ring? Or, maybe they are just mentally sick people!"

As the light turns green, the women drive off without giving Frankie his tip. He shouts out, "You little cheapskates. No wonder you are driving that old banger that looks like it came out of a cereal box!"

Ozzy watches all this with amusement. Commie looks at his factometer and shakes his head once again. His *reality check* shows that the car belonged to Mrs. Angela Fuller, the older woman, who was a widow suffering from deafness. She had declared personal bankruptcy the previous year. The woman sitting next to her was Samantha Truman, a one-time supermodel who was completely paralysed from head to foot due to a car accident. The poor woman had been left with a permanent awkward smile on her face, as a result of the paralysis. The little girl in the back seat was Trudie, Samantha's niece. The two women were driving Trudy back to her mother's home in New Jersey. The weather was very hot and the car had no air conditioning, causing the poor child to cry because she could not bear the heat! Neither of the women could do anything to help her, for one was deaf and the other was paralysed! Commie beams a message to Ozzy, which says, *"Negative polarisation* again!"

It is now time for Frankie to take a break. He wanders over to a coffee shop across the street and orders himself his usual giant American coffee mug. His girlfriend Rachel joins him and the two chat over their super-sized coffees. Ozzy and Commie follow them intently. Frankie proceeds to tell Rachel about the Mercedes 990 and Pontiac Polaris. Rachel says to Frankie, "It is possible that you could be wrong about both those situations. You cannot be sure about what was really happening in the lives of those people"

Frankie replies, "Rachel, I know people when I see them and I am usually right about them."

Rachel then says, "Frankie, you always tend to see the negative aspects in everyone and everything, and form instantaneous opinions about people. That is your problem, my dear sweetheart."

Frankie's defences rise immediately. He snaps back, "Rachel, this world is full of bad, sick people. I mean, just look at the news every day. We live in a dog-eat-dog world. If you dwell on the negative side of things, you'll be right eight times out of ten!"

Rachel replies, "It is not about being right or wrong. None of us has the authority or the true knowledge to judge others. In every situation, there is a positive and a negative. Why can't we accept both sides and avoid judging people or forming harsh opinions? What if we just remained *neutral?"*

Frankie replies, "What you say is interesting, but from my experience, there are a lot more bad people in the world than there are good ones."

Rachel, who is not impressed with Frankie's argument, asks, "How do you truly know who is good and who is bad? Why do you always need to classify people? Why can't they just be people — simply people? Why can't you accept them for what they are? Why can't our lives be based on simple *acceptance* of everything?"

Frankie is beginning to enjoy this conversation. His sweetheart Rachel is turning philosophical on him! He replies, "Rachel, what you say makes sense. But, I have been hurt so much in the past by people. I can't help feeling the way I do."

With an understanding smile, Rachel replies, "Frankie, I don't doubt that you have been hurt by many people before. Have you ever thought about whether it was they who hurt you, or whether it was you who hurt yourself due to your negativity about everything? I mean, look at your best friend Jimmy. You never appreciated anything that he did for you. You were always suspicious of his motives. You always thought he had a hidden agenda. Rather than thank him for the things he did for you, you always criticised him for the things he didn't do for you. The two of you were partners and friends and together, you built up a successful business. But you could never trust anyone. You spent more time looking behind your back to see who was going to stab you than looking forward and building on what you had both started. Jimmy was different. He gave all he had to the business and to your friendship. He tried very hard to get through to you that everything in this world is not negative. He brought such wonderful opportunities to the company but you were too pessimistic to take them on. You feared failure in everything. You had failed without even trying, or without even giving yourself the chance to try. I can't blame Jimmy for dissolving the partnership. He is doing well in building up his share of the business again. Yet here we are, living on the streets. Frankie, haven't you learned anything from all that has happened? Can't you see that it was your negativity and pessimism that has landed you where you are today?"

Frankie listens to all this quietly. He cannot disagree with what Rachel had said. He then comments, "Rachel, all my life, I have been afraid of everything. I have feared people, events and everything. All I have felt is hurt from the actions of people who have come into my life. I was very hurt when Jimmy dissolved our partnership. I felt completely betrayed. Yet, as I listen to you speak, I begin to wonder whether or not I have brought all this upon myself. I mean, I have even forgotten what it feels like to smile!"

Rachel sees that Frankie is getting very emotional. She says to him, "Frankie, I believe that most of your pain has been self-inflicted. When you only see the negative and when you live in paranoia, even tiny problems become huge avalanches that cause you so much pain. Frankie, a problem can be as big as you want it to be, or it can be as small as you want it to be. Seeing the dark side of things makes us live in darkness. This darkness affects all those around us. It causes our friends and loved ones to either reject us completely or to remain guarded about how they deal with us. Therefore, they appear to us to be the bad guys. This *perception* feeds on itself and grows until we cannot accept brightness in anything. My dear Frankie, look where all this has brought you. I mean, what if someone could tell you the truth behind your two experiences today; about the Mercedes and the Pontiac? What if you discovered that you were completely wrong?"

Frankie replies, "I would love to know the facts in both cases."

Rachel continues, "Frankie, learn to accept people and events. Learn to go with the flow. Accept the fact that there is no good and no bad. Become *neutral*."

Ozzy and Commie sat through this whole conversation, dumbfounded. In a single conversation, Rachel had proved more than their fancy experiment with the perceptometer and the factometer ever could. If only Frankie could see how different *perception* can be from *reality*. He would be so much happier!

Commie, who has an entrepreneurial spark in him, says, "Ozzy, we should sell our perceptometer and factometer to the people of the earth. It would make them so much wiser, don't you think so?"

Ozzy replies with a chuckle, "Yes, but then they would come to colonise us!"

Leaving Frankie and Rachel, Ozzy and Commie start to look for other subjects to study. Commie says to Ozzy, "Rachel was dead right when she said that the best way to live life is to have an attitude of *acceptance* and *neutrality*. I mean, that's how we all live our lives on Mars."

Ozzy replies, "You see, human beings need to evolve further in order to overcome the limitations of their polarised thinking and perceptions. This has been the cause of many wars, conflict, destruction and unhappiness in countless of their civilisations. But they will evolve..."

THE VISIT TO HARVARD

A few hours later, Ozzy and Commie arrive at the Harvard Business School campus in Boston. They look around at the lecture rooms, libraries, students' centre and sports facilities. They find Harvard rather intriguing, as it is so different from their own university. Ozzy says to Commie, "This is where they create the best business brains on earth. Well, at least that is what I read in my encyclopaedia at home. They follow a model of teaching based on what they call 'case studies.' They examine the ways in which real companies actually transact business. The students study failures and successes and learn valuable lessons from how things were done. They also develop ideas on how things should be done in the future. This is a good form of education, I feel."

Commie replies, "For this model of teaching or learning to work, it is essential that the teachers and students not be *polarised*. They should have the ability to look at the *positive* and *negative polarities* in every situation. Then, from a position of *neutrality*, as Rachel beautifully put it, they will be able to learn the most."

Commie continues, "Why don't we test some of the students here, Ozzy? We have some time on our hands."

Ozzy agrees and the two Martians comb the Harvard campus in search of candidates to test. In the main library, they see Professor Cheryl Bose, a specialist on the Power of Positive Thinking. She is well known around the world. She has written many books on the subject and lectured at numerous international conferences. Ozzy says to Commie, "After Frankie, this candidate should be interesting. I feel certain that she is going to be very different."

Ozzy takes his spot in her brain, with his perceptometer all set up. Commie then follows Cheryl with his factometer as she heads out towards the lecture theatre to give a group of around 50 students a lesson on positive thinking. She starts her talk by saying, "Today, we are going to study the importance of positive thinking. We are going to look at a case study of the famous Hong Kong entrepreneur, Simon Lee. As you all know, entrepreneurs are a unique breed of people. They believe in themselves and are optimistic about everything. When you give them a glass of water that is filled halfway, they will immediately tell you that the glass is half full. Others, who think differently, would say it is half empty. Both of course are correct, but the way people *perceive* things is clearly reflected in how they behave, make decisions and lead their lives. Simon is definitely one who sees the glass as half full. He runs a clothing company that manufactures mid-market-priced fashions in Asia and exports them to North America. He started this company with $2,000 and has grown it to a $200-million empire. But Simon wants to grow even further. He has only one philosophy, 'Nothing is impossible. Everything can be done.' So far, he has succeeded with this philosophy, often to the frustration of his management team. Now he wants to expand the size of his company by acquiring the Nimiko fashion conglomerate in

Japan. Nimiko has sales of one billion dollars per year, which is five times the level of sales of Simon's company. Simon has hired top investment bankers to study the deal. They are, however, divided in their opinion as to what Simon should do. The no-can-do camp says that the deal is too risky for Simon because Nimiko is too large and also because it's corporate culture is very different to Simon's company. Over the years, Simon has surrounded himself with aggressive, commando-style people, who would stop at nothing to reach their objectives. By contrast, Nimiko's corporate culture is more hierarchical and slow. Nimiko grew to one billion in sales over a 20-year period. Simon reached $200 million in sales in three years. The cultures of the two organisations are obviously very different. In addition, the no-can-do camp feels that the fashion market is changing too quickly and that the new competition from Mainland China would pose a threat to Simon's business if he took over Nimiko. Simon has listened carefully to all these arguments."

She continues, "Then, there is the can-do camp that says that the take-over would instantly give Simon an empire that had over one billion dollars in sales. It would put him in a new league, with the big boys. They argue that corporate culture is not a problem, since Simon could introduce his philosophies into Nimiko's old-guard management style. It would take some time but it could be done. They also argue that Simon could better face the Mainland Chinese competition if he ran a bigger company with a power base in Japan. Now, Simon has a decision to make. What is it going to be, ladies and gentlemen?"

Ozzy and Commie exchange signals to one another. Both are curious to see where this session leads. The Professor has laid out the case very clearly. Now the class has to come up with ideas as to what Simon should do. Later, the Professor will tell them what he actually did and what the outcome was. The Martians are fascinated. It seems like their instruments are not really needed here.

A 40-year-old student by the name of Gerry takes the floor. He says, "Simon should not do this deal. Whilst he may be able to handle the instant change in organisation size, he will never be able to break the cultural barriers of Nimiko. Remember that he is the little guy and they are the big boys. Remember also that Japanese culture in itself is so different and regimented, compared to Hong Kong. This transaction would destroy everything Simon has built so far because he is trying to mix oil with water. As for the Mainland Chinese competition, they will accelerate his demise if he does take over Nimiko."

The Professor thinks about this argument from Simon's perspective. He was an entrepreneur with a very positive outlook. How would he react to Gerry's position? Could he handle an instantaneous quintupling in the size of his company? His positive mind would say, "Yes, of course." Could he break the cultural barriers? He would probably say, "Yes of course. Nothing is impossible." Could he work his way through the Chinese competition? He would probably say, "Let's take them on. The more the merrier!" Professor Cheryl's own personal thoughts are in line with Simon's except that she is more guarded by nature. Ozzy picks up Cheryl's thoughts very quickly and passes them on to Commie.

Then Carla, a 30-year-old student, stands up and says, "Simon should not go for this transaction. He has built a company step-by-step, from $2,000 to $200 million in sales. This is the path he knows. Running a $1.2-billion company overnight may be something he knows nothing about. Why should he take such a risk?"

The Professor replies, "Carla, when he started with $2,000, he did not know anything about running a $200 million company. He did well getting that far because he was not afraid of taking on challenges. So, why should this one be any different? After all, it is only a matter of size, isn't it?"

Carla replies, "He has charted unknown waters before, but this challenge is in a new league."

Then Jamie, a 28-year-old student from Chile, comments, "I think he should go for the deal believing in his capability to overcome the challenges of instant growth, culture and competition. Simon is a great example of an entrepreneur with a strong positive outlook. He should go for it."

Then, a lady by the name of Zaheeda from Pakistan interjects with the question, "Why does he have to grow at all? Why does he need to do this deal? Simon is now 50 years old. My research tells me that he suffers from heart disease. Why should he spend the next ten years of his life battling such a huge challenge? At the end of the day, what is in it for him as a person?"

This question renders the whole class silent. Strangely, everyone had started with the assumption, "There is a deal to be done here." Everyone dived into analysing the polarities, i.e. the pros and cons. Everyone's thinking was focussed on the business aspects of the transaction. Yet, here was a fundamental question from the heart that touched on a pure human dimension. Even though the cultural aspects that were discussed thus far had a humanistic dimension, the overall analysis had been based on a purely business perspective — a win-or-lose approach.

The professor breaks the silence by saying, "Zaheeda raises an interesting point. How does a strong, positive-minded person answer such a question? How does a pessimist answer such a question?"

Zaheeda replies, "It all has to do with one's *road map* of life. Entrepreneurs like Simon are driven by the desire to grow and succeed. They want to make small things big and big things bigger. Many of them do not have a *road map* that addresses such questions as, 'What am I doing this for? Is this what I want from my life? What is my reward for the price I have to pay?' These are important issues that merit consideration."

The Professor replies, "Simon would probably say that he is doing it for the satisfaction."

Zaheeda inquires, "At what point does he feel that satisfaction — at the beginning, mid-way or at the end? Is there ever an end? When does he earn the reward of satisfaction? Is it an end result? Is it a destination? I think life itself is a journey, not a destination. So where is Simon's journey taking him?"

Zaheeda's questions have found a place deep in the minds and hearts of the class. They have also sparked the famous professor's thinking about *road maps*. She then says, "For the past two hours, we have analysed the pros and cons of the take-over of Nimiko by Simon. Some of you have argued that he should not do the deal and some of you have argued that he should. We have all recognised Simon's bias towards the positive, which is *positive polarisation*. Yet, Zaheeda's suggestion about the *road map* comes from a point of *neutrality*. It is neither positive nor negative, but it seeks to explore the *purpose* of everything from a personal, human dimension. This is very interesting because with a well defined *road map*, people like Simon, and everyone else for that matter, would achieve a great deal more in their lives."

The professor continues, "I am sure you all want to know what happened to Simon. Well, he did take over Nimiko successfully. He managed to deal with the instant growth well. But, he failed to deal with the huge cultural differences that existed between his young dynamic group and the old, entrenched Japanese culture. Time was not on his side. While it took Simon three years to build a $200-million company starting with only $2,000, he lost his entire fortune over the next two years. But, knowing Simon, he is strong and positive and he will build again. This time, he will be wiser. I am sure all of you have learnt by now that being positive alone is not sufficient. One needs *wisdom*, and interestingly enough, this *wisdom* comes from the *zone of neutrality* that Zaheeda talked about. Simon possessed all the powers of positive thinking. But, he was completely unfamiliar with the *zone of neutrality* from where *wisdom* can be drawn. Remember, class, the world's most successful people have failed at least three times before making it to the top. The same is probably true for everyone, because while achievements vary in monetary or material size, everybody has their own mansion to build. But, I think that the failures, if properly understood and analysed, take people to *neutrality*. From there, they rise to greater heights in whatever they do. Unfortunately, for most people, failure or loss takes them further out on the negative side, towards negative polarisation. Such people never truly grow again, until they find neutrality. Therefore, when we study people, events and cases, we should always bear in mind that the third zone, which is the *neutral zone*, merits the same degree of attention as the *positive* and *negative polarities.*"

Ozzy and Commie are impressed. What a lesson! Now they can understand why Frankie ended up washing windshields, when at one time he had a partnership that could have gone places had he not been so negative and pessimistic. Rachel had shown him the *neutral zone* over their coffee discussion. Then, at Harvard Business School, there was the fascinating case study of Simon, who played in the big leagues, but still needed to discover and understand the ever-important *neutral zone.*

It is no surprise that the research report that Ozzy and Commie presented to their professors and peers back in Mars was entitled, "The Neutral Zone."

Seeds of Resolution

❋ Let us take a few moments to reflect on our own *polarity*. We should seek to discover, with complete self-honesty, whether we are *positively* or *negatively polarised*.

❋ We need to reflect on our past and recent experiences to recognise what role our *polarity* has played in the creation of these experiences.

❋ We should aim to regularly contemplate the *neutral zone*, by repeating the words:

"I AM AT EQUILIBRIUM. I AM NEUTRAL."

❋ These words will help us to internalise the importance of achieving equilibrium in all that we do. They will also serve as a constant reminder that there is always a difference between *perception* and *reality*.

❋ When we have fully recognised the impact of *polarity*, we will be able to better understand those around us and take the first steps toward enjoying greater fulfilment in all our relationships.

My Reflections

Now   date: / / .

My Reflections

One Year Hence   date: / / .

My Reflections

Evolution *is a concept that has been discussed and debated extensively throughout history, particularly when attempting to explain the origins of the human race and the environment. The Theory of Evolution, for example, suggests that life originated in the ocean from single cell forms, which changed and evolved into multi-cellular organisms and, over time, gave rise to the multitude of species that we see on land, air and in water. The essence of this theory is "change." Every change in the environment or surroundings of an organism causes it to naturally adapt itself accordingly. This process of adaptation is called "evolution", which results in new and different versions of the original organism.* Evolution *is a natural process.*

From the perspective of achieving zero conflict, *it is very important to understand the role and necessity of* evolution. *Most changes yield* conflicts. *The process of* evolution, *however, enables adaptation to changes, with little or no conflict.* Evolution *allows changes to take their natural course, which in essence eliminates conflict. The opposite of evolution is* "intervention", *which involves artificially influencing a process of change in order to cause or force its direction in a manner that may be in conflict with its natural course. Intervention is a source of immense* conflict, *both within us and within our environment. In terms of attitude, the word* evolution *subscribes to the phrase* "let it be," *whereas,* intervention *subscribes to the phrase* "cause it to be." *The key difference between the two phrases lies in the words* let *and* cause.

THE PROMISE OF THE ROSE

There was once a charming 12-year-old girl whose name was Sarah. She lived in the southwest of England, in a mansion that was surrounded by a beautiful garden, which consisted of plants and flowers, particularly roses, from all over the world. It was a famous place that was visited by people from all around England. Sarah loved roses. She often spent hours walking amongst the rose beds that were endowed with flowers of a wide array of colours, shapes and sizes.

One morning, as Sarah was walking past a rose bush with her grandfather, she stopped to look at a splendid rosebud that had just begun to blossom at its tip. She marvelled at the perfectly compacted petals that were waiting to open and reveal their beauty to the world. She plucked the rosebud and continued to look at its beautiful red tip. She could not wait to see all the other petals that were hidden inside this intriguing rosebud. She proceeded to peel back the green leaf-cover of the bud and paused to look at the petals that were tightly packed together. She then began to pull each petal open, one by one. To her dismay, the petals began to fall off the bud and a few moments later, they were blown away by the wind. By the time she had opened up the rosebud, it did not look like a flower at all. The promise of a beautiful rose that was hidden in the rosebud was lost. Instead, what Sarah ended up with was a green and brown stub around which only a few petals survived. All the rest of the petals were gone. Sarah was most disappointed.

Her grandfather, George, who had observed this episode patiently, then said, "Sarah, what you have in your hands is no longer a rose! Why did you forcefully peel the rosebud open?"

Sarah replied, "Grandpa, when I saw the rosebud, I imagined it would reveal one of the most beautiful roses in the garden when it blossomed, but I could not wait for the bud to blossom by itself, so I tried to open the petals myself. Now, there is no rose. There is only a sad-looking stump. I feel cheated and disappointed. The petals that are left on this stump do not even have the beautiful scent that the roses in this garden normally possess."

George smiled at his granddaughter and said, "Sarah, if you were patient and allowed the rosebud to blossom by itself, you would have been shown the most beautiful rose in the garden. Its scent would have surpassed all the roses in this garden. What you should have done was to allow the bud to blossom by itself. You should have allowed it to *evolve*. You should have *let it be*. Then you would have discovered the full promise of the splendid rosebud."

George continued, "Instead of waiting to allow the rosebud to *evolve* into a flower, you *intervened*. You forced the bud to open up, and in doing so, it lost all its petals. The scent was not allowed to manifest either. Therefore, my dear Sarah, you destroyed the rosebud, and its promise of the flower to come, through *intervention*. You tried to *'cause it to be'* rather than *'let it be'*. This intervention has led to your disappointment."

Sarah kissed the stump of what had been a beautiful rosebud a few moments previously, and said, "I am sorry to have destroyed you. I am sorry for my impatience. I sincerely hope that someday you will become a rosebud again and reveal to me your promise."

George then said, "Sarah, today you have learnt an important lesson. In your life, do not try to *intervene* in things, events, and the lives of people, for in doing so, you will destroy many a beautiful promise. Keep away from *intervention*, my dear. Learn to *let things be*. Learn to let things *evolve*. It is only through *evolution* that you will be able to discover all the wonderful promises of life."

Twenty-five years later, Sarah remembered her grandfather's words as she walked through the rose garden. She was now a mother of two lovely children, a 13-year-old boy and a 7-year-old girl. Her children were happy and well nurtured. She had brought them up in accordance with her grandfather's advice. She had *let them evolve*. She did *not intervene*. Sarah was a smart woman. She knew where to draw the line with her children when it came to discipline. Yet, she offered them a loving, nurturing environment in which they were allowed to *evolve* and blossom. She sadly remembered her 16-year-old nephew, Albert, who had run away from his home a year earlier. Sarah had engaged in many heated discussions with her sister, Emily, on the issue of Albert's upbringing.

Emily and her husband, Bill, had placed immense pressures on Albert, ever since he was a toddler. They expected too much from him. He was pushed hard into being a perfect child who achieved top results at school; displayed best behaviour at all times; and emulated the personality of his father, who was a very successful lawyer. Sarah often told Emily about the story of the rosebud. She cautioned Emily against her strong *intervention* in Albert's life. She urged Emily and Bill to let Albert *evolve, to let him be*. But, her advice and caution fell upon deaf ears. Albert was forcefully being moulded into a "Bill junior." Albert could not cope with being pressured by his parents and ultimately turned to taking drugs. Then, one day, he ran away from home. Poor Albert was like the rosebud Sarah had once destroyed through her *intervention*. Now that he was gone, Sarah dreaded the thought that she may never see him again. She heard her late grandfather's voice ring out within her, saying, *"Evolution is the way — let it be."*

Each time we try to fulfil our desires by forcing events through *intervention*, we create conflict, pressure and stress. These are sources of negative feelings and emotions, which often manifest in the form of hurt, anger and frustration. If we can learn to *let it be*, then we will be able to "go with the flow" through our lives, thus eliminating unnecessary pain, pressure, anger and stress. An enlightened teacher once said, "We should learn not to mould events to fit our desires. Rather, we should let our desires follow the events." This is indeed the path of *evolution*.

We encounter the lessons from the story of Sarah every day of our lives, in all the events of the day, be they small or large events. As we look at ourselves or our loved ones and friends, we should ask ourselves, "Am I *letting them be?* Am I allowing them to *evolve?* Am I *intervening* in their lives?" We should remember that *intervention* often starts with good intentions, but the outcome can be devastating, nevertheless. When we are faced with decisions to make, we should ask ourselves, "Will my actions *intervene* or will they allow *evolution?*" This thought process does not imply that we should avoid helping our fellow beings for fear that we may be *intervening* in their lives. There is no harm in offering help or advice to others, as long is we do so without exerting undue pressure on them. It is important to recognise that allowing things to *evolve* embodies a peace in itself, which comes from the absence of conflict.

During the extensive gardening lessons that Sarah received from her grandfather, George, she was also taught the wisdom of how to bring about positive change, while maintaining harmony with *evolution*. One day, Sarah and George were looking at a plant in the shed, which George wanted to grow into a miniature tree. The problem was that the stem of the plant was growing sideways, while George wanted it to grow vertically. He said to Sarah, "You see my dear, if I bend the stem to make it grow vertically, I will break it. So, I am going to move this plant and position it directly underneath the skylight in the roof. The stem will then automatically grow vertically towards the sunlight. In this way, I will have allowed it to evolve in the right direction. You see Sarah, I will have *intervened* in the direction of its growth, but I will have done so by respecting the principle of *evolution*."

This simple example of George's plant in the shed teaches us that we can help effect positive change and yet *let things be*. Therefore, *evolution* does not necessarily mean, "all hands off." Understanding and carefully controlling *intervention* is the key to avoiding conflict. Allowing *evolution* leads to the completion of every process or cycle in life, in a manner that reveals the wonderful promises that we deserve to discover.

THE SPANISH BODEGA

Stress and pressure are amongst the most commonly used words of our time. They are indeed the sources of many conflicts, health problems, disappointments and difficulties. These stresses primarily come from strong *interventions* that we exert on our own lives and on the lives of those whom we encounter. We often pass on our stress to others, resulting in pain and frustration in their lives. If we truly understand *evolution*, and keep our interventions in check, we will be able to eliminate a significant proportion of the unhealthy stress and pressure in our lives. If we are the recipients of damaging stress from others, we should address the causative issues with them quickly in order to seek healthy resolutions. If this is not possible and we find ourselves being constantly dragged down by stresses from such people, we should consider avoiding them as best as we can, but in a polite and friendly manner. This form of avoidance does not mean that we are running away from our problematic relationships. It simply means that we are learning to manage our relationships in a manner that always allows us the time and space devoid of the damaging stress, which then helps to bring out the best in us. In this regard, the following simple incident was quite an eye-opener for me:

One day, I watched a group of men and women enjoying a bottle of wine as they sat around a wooden bench in a bodega in Andalusia, Spain. The man, who looked like the host of the party, kept pouring wine into the glasses of his guests until the bottle was empty. It was clear that he truly enjoyed sharing this bottle with his friends. A few minutes later, in the midst of the conversation, he picked up the bottle once more to pour from it. I watched his face as it dawned on him that the bottle was empty. His smile disappeared for a moment. I sensed that he was disappointed that there was no more wine left for him to share with his friends. Perhaps it was the last bottle of that particular brand of wine available in the bodega. He looked towards me for a brief moment. I smiled at him and said, "You cannot pour from an empty bottle." There is an important message in this story for us all to grasp. *Only when you are full can you fulfil.* If we allow ourselves to be constantly drained by the stresses of others around us, then we too may become like the empty bottle. We may not be left with much to give of ourselves. Hence, intelligently controlling the rate at which we get drained is an important aspect of managing our lives as we strive *towards zero conflict*. This is in keeping with the laws of *evolution*.

We must also recognise that not all types of stress and pressure are bad for us. Some represent healthy and motivating energies, for example, healthy competition, which must be harnessed. However, distinguishing between healthy and unhealthy stresses in our lives is a personal matter, which requires careful consideration.

Seeds of Resolution

❋ Let us contemplate and internalise the following seeds:

"LET IT BE.
LET ALL THINGS EVOLVE..."

❋ These words carry an energy and peace that helps to shape our attitudes towards everything in our lives.

❋ They provide the soothing ointment that helps us mend and maintain our relationships with our friends and loved ones.

❋ They empower us to maximise our potential in everything that we do.

❋ When we are in the midst of turmoil and difficulty, we may be able to find solutions to our problems by identifying and understanding our *interventions*, and correcting them accordingly.

❋ At the end of each day, we should reflect upon the intentions underlying our deeds. We should ask ourselves how much we *intervened* in all that occurred around us. We should ask ourselves whether our *interventions* were in keeping with the laws of *evolution*. This is an essential step *towards zero conflict*.

My Reflections

Now   date: / /   .

My Reflections

One Year Hence   date: / / .

Chapter 7

EXPECTATIONS

*Learn to count the blessings that you have,
for they are really yours. And,
do not grieve for what you do not have
for they are not yours.*

Expectations *are in-built desires that drive us to try and shape the outcome of events that lie ahead of us.* Expectations *govern, to a large extent, how we feel, act and treat those around us. We are all conditioned to expect events to unfold in a manner that meets with our desires, or for people to act towards us or perform in a manner that we find acceptable.* Expectations *keep us living in the future rather than in the present. Our expectations and how we go about pursuing them can be a significant source of* conflict, *both within ourselves and with those around us.*

The following story from my first book, Reflections from the Origin *relates an interesting insight into human expectations.*

THE MIRAGE

It was early morning. The sun had begun to rise. I had been running around in the forest for days, not knowing where I was going. Each time I reached what looked like a path that was going somewhere, there were at least four different directions I could take. I looked to the sky, for the sun to guide me. But the forest was so dense that I could not see the sun. I knew it was daytime, but the sun just seemed to be like a distant haze over the leaves of the trees. I did not know how long I had been wandering in this forest. I was desperate to get out of it. I would have given anything for a drink of cool, fresh water. I could not recall the number of crossroads that I had encountered in the forest. All I knew was that there were many. And, for all I knew, I could have been travelling in circles for days! Maybe I was where I had started. Or maybe I was a long way away! I wished that someone would show up to guide me. But, from where? And, in such a dense forest, with no distinct landmarks, how could anyone find their way? Just then, I looked at the ground and the soil started to appear white in colour. My heart beat with excitement! Then I heard the sound of flowing water — there was a river close by. I yearned for this beautiful sound. I would have given anything for it! And then, the sound got closer as I came to a clearing in the forest. The soil was now completely white and I looked at this beautiful river, whose crystal-clear water glittered in the morning sun. It was like a golden serpent. The water frolicked over the rocks playfully, inviting me to rush to it and drink to my heart's content. I ran towards the water and threw my hands out to scoop up this precious blessing. My thirst had reached an unbearable level. But then, suddenly, I found myself thrusting my hands into hot burning sand! All I scooped out to rinse my face with was hot burning sand! What had happened? Where was the cool water that I had so dearly desired? Where was the river? Where were the frolicking ripples? I felt cheated. I felt angry. I felt a rage that could have made me destroy everything around me. Even if a guide had shown up now, I could have killed him or her.

I ran around screaming and pounding my feet on the burning sand. I looked into the sky and saw the sun shining down on me for the first time in days. I could have cared less! I had forgotten the misery I had felt in the forest when I could not find the sun. It was now visible, but I felt completely indifferent. A few moments earlier I would have given anything to find the sun, for then I could have been guided by its position in the sky and could have enjoyed its warm rays that would have brought life and warmth to my cold, damp, weary cheeks.

I cried out to the Origin, my Creator, "How cruel can You be? After showing me the river and raising all my hopes, You took it away! How cruel can You get? They all said that You were merciful. That is not true! In the name of the Heavens, it is not true!" I sat in the sand and wept.

Then I heard a loud, clear and powerful Voice say to me, *"I am not the One that is cruel. There was never a river. It was a mirage that you had created in your mind. It was something that you had wanted so dearly that, behold, by the power of the intellect that I have given to you, you created the illusion of a river! It was only a mirage. Had I willed that the river be there, I would simply say, 'Be,' and it would Be. But, my dear one, your anger and disappointment are nothing but your own folly."*

The Voice continued, *"When you desire something so much, you force everything around you to fit your desires. You must learn to 'Let it Be'. Do not force events and circumstances in your life to meet your desires. That will make you unhappy, as you are now. Look at yourself, you look miserable! Learn to let your desires follow the events and not the reverse. Had you done so, you would now be very happy, for after days of wandering, I have led you to the sun! A drink of cool water could never have led you out of this forest, which you found so miserable. But the sun would have! Learn to recognise the signs that I have placed around you to see and follow. Some things in life bring short-term, immediate gratification, like the sip of the cool river water that you had so desired. Yet, you really were not going to die without water because the leaves of the forest that fed you also gave you all the water that* you needed. Yet, look at you, how angry and hurt you are. What you really needed was the clearing in the forest so that the sun and stars could guide you back to your home. I knew better what you needed. Yet now that you have received what you so desperately needed, you do not recognise it with gratitude! Instead, you call Me cruel for what you did not find! The reason you could not find the river was that it never existed. You chased a mirage."

The Voice continued, "My dear one, learn to count the blessings that you have, for they are really yours. And, do not grieve for what you do not have for they are not yours. Do not mould all your circumstances and events to fit your desires, for more often than not, all you will find is a mirage. But, if you place your trust in Me, and follow My guidance, you will find that your desires will follow the events, and you will find what is truly important, like the sun that you have just discovered. Live your life in this way and the anger, pain and grief that you feel right now will touch you no more! Celebrate this day, for you have been guided and shown a way out of this forest! And remember, tomorrow there will be another forest..."

When we think about *expectations*, we need to be able to separate our *needs* from our *wants*. Here is an exercise that will help us to achieve this:

Make a list of all the things in your life that you absolutely could not live without, and would not trade for anything else. This is your list of *needs*, which may include people, events and material things. In essence, this list should have items that would severely impinge on the quality of your life if you could not have them.

Now, list all the things that you would like to, or would absolutely love to have. Once again, this list may include people, events and material things. This list should be such that if any item on it were not available to you, you would still be able to carry on with your life, albeit, somewhat disappointed. This is your *wants* list.

This simple exercise may help us start to differentiate our *needs* from our *wants*. We may also be able to start seeing where the *mirages* in our lives exist. Let us reflect on what the Origin said in the above story, *"Learn to count the blessings that you have, for they are really yours. And, do not grieve for what you do not have, for they are not yours."* Clearly, one major source of inner conflict and unhappiness in our lives is our *wants*. We forget to recognise and appreciate what we have. Instead, we focus on what we do not have, that others around us may have, and then feel very unhappy and inadequate. Sometimes, our *wants* become obsessions that completely engross our lives, resulting in serious conflicts within ourselves and with those around us. It is important for us to recognise these obsessions, for they certainly reside in our minds as *mirages*, which may ultimately disappoint and hurt us. It is important for us to try to let go of these obsessions. As we start to focus on what we do have, rather than on what we do not have, we may begin to experience inner contentment, which will help us to detach ourselves from our *wants*. We will also begin to realise that, as in the story of the "Mirage," the sun has indeed shone upon us over and over again — we just failed to recognise it.

Detaching from our *wants* does not mean shying away from our goals and ambitions.. Of course, we must all have goals and ambitions to pursue. That is an essential aspect of living.

However, learning to detach ourselves from our *wants* will help us to gain a healthier, more balanced and neutral perspective, with respect to our goals and ambitions. If we become detached from them, we will be able to view them more objectively, plan them more carefully and implement them in a sensible, mature and compassionate manner, in the absence of distracting emotions. Such detachment prevents the formation of *mirages*, which are illusions. Chasing illusions can be a painful, frustrating and an utterly non-productive exercise.

THE ATHLETE

As we reflect more carefully about our *expectations*, we will gradually become more realistic about them. When I look at my children, they are all different. I have a son who is capable of achieving A's in most of his subjects and my *expectation* of him revolve around my perception of his capabilities. My daughter, on the other hand, is not an A student. She works extremely hard and manages to achieve B's and C's. Clearly, I would be placing undue hardship upon her if I were to *expect* A's from her. She would need to give up the blessing of being a child in order to work even harder to try to meet my unfair *expectations*, which may eventually lead to devastating consequences, I may add. My daughter excels in other aspects of her life, where my son is rather weak. Therefore, each child comes into this world with his or her own unique gifts. As parents, our role is to help them shine and excel with those precious gifts. Placing unrealistic *expectations* upon our children destroys this wonderful process, often resulting in hurt and disappointments that can last an entire lifetime. As parents, we should reflect upon our own childhoods to realise the truth embodied in these statements.

My son is a great athlete. Each time he goes for a 100-metre track competition, I look forward to and *want* to see him come home with a gold medal. Yet, as I place myself in his shoes, I realise that he is competing against the best athletes from other schools. Therefore, there is a pretty good chance that he may not win the gold medal, but at least I will know that he will have done his best in training and preparing for the competition. The last thing he would need is pressure from me by saying, "Come back with the gold medal." He should not be made to feel that he would disappoint me should he not win the gold medal. Rather, he should be made to feel confident to go out there and do his best. If he does not win, then he must know that I am there to comfort him and help him to do better next time. Clearly, I can only think this way because my *expectations* of him are fair and reasonable. This is because, in this case, my *wants* are not governing my *expectations*. My son has a number of weaknesses as well, in other aspects of his life, and my *expectations* of him in those areas are different. Since I understand my *expectations* of him, I am able to assist and guide him to realise his full potential, without placing unfair pressure on him. My son and I have a wonderful relationship because of the manner in which I approach his personal development. He and I work together to harness his true potential. Every parent *wants* his or her child to be perfect. Many of us place immense pressures on our children because of these *wants*. While some pressure is healthy, our unrealistic *expectations* sometimes can cause permanent damage in our relationships with our children. Our love, affection and acceptance towards our children should never be conditional upon their meeting our *expectations*. This concept of *expectations* can be extrapolated to our spouses, loved ones, friends and colleagues.

Expectations can be a major source of conflict in all dimensions of our lives. Whilst having *expectations* is an essential aspect of our existence, clearly understanding our *expectations* and placing them within a correct context takes us a long way towards eliminating conflict. An important bonus for us in this process is the experience of contentment and happiness that comes from successfully putting our *needs* and *wants* in their correct places.

Seeds of Resolution

❊ Let us set aside some time regularly to review the list of our *needs* and *wants*. The very process of reflecting upon these lists helps us to take major strides towards finding peace within ourselves, because we will be putting everything in our lives into a clearer perspective.

❊ When we look at our list of *needs*, we should be grateful when we recognise that we do indeed have most of the things we *need* in life. This recognition in itself is a source of positive energy that brings tranquillity and a sense of self-security.

❊ When we look at our list of *wants*, we should repeat to ourselves:

"This is not important. It does not make me, nor does it break me."

This will enable us to start building a healthy detachment from our *wants*.

❊ Interestingly enough, this detachment will actually help us to achieve some of our *wants* with greater ease. We learnt about *Flow* in Chapter 4. This detachment will help us to *flow* with complete flexibility towards achieving some of our *wants*. It will also help us to identify the *mirages* that we should avoid. After all, life is too short to waste precious time and energy chasing illusions.

❊ When we find ourselves feeling frustrated or disappointed about something, we should pause for a few moments, sit quietly by ourselves, and ask the question, *"Is it a need or a want?"* The very process of stepping away from the issue and examining it in this manner will help to bring clarity in our thinking. We can then decide on how best to deal with the matter.

My Reflections

Now   date: / / .

My Reflections

One Year Hence   date: / / .

Chapter 8

MOTIVATIONS

*"Motivation is a driving
force that gives birth
to events and experiences
in the arena of life"*

113

Everything we do in our daily life is driven by our motivations. As human beings, we need a driving force to make us go places, achieve things and gain all the wonderful experiences that life has to offer. We set our goals and objectives each day, and then we try our level best to fulfil these expectations, but the inner driving force that ultimately causes us to act is "motivation". Whilst motivation is very healthy, it can also be a source of significant inner and outer conflict if it is not properly understood and harnessed. There are two principal types of motivation, namely, "negative motivation" and "positive motivation". Examples of some of our motivations include: competition, success, failure, greed, jealousy, hatred, revenge, fear, pride, oppression, submission, ambition, love, generosity, obedience, defiance, humility, friendship, power, influence, protection and respect. Motivations arise from basic instincts, such as hunger or sex, and from simple or complex emotions, some of which have been mentioned above. Of course, it would not be possible for us to examine every type of motivation within the scope of this book. However, it is useful to look at certain examples of positive and negative motivations in order to develop a process by which we can identify, understand, and manage our inner driving forces.

THE COLISEUM

"Competition can be a positive or a negative motivation depending upon how it is approached."

114

The year is 106 AD. A large crowd has gathered at the Coliseum in Rome, to watch a contest between two gladiators, Hector and Lance. The Emperor Tyrus is presiding over the contest, accompanied by his beautiful wife, the Empress Liana. The winner of the contest is the gladiator who survives.

Hector is the son of a peasant who grew up in the outer fields of Rome. He lost his father when he was only eight years old and was brought up by his mother, Angela, who taught him to till the land, grow crops and sell them in the market place. Hector was a very responsible child and he assumed the role of the father in the family, despite his tender, young age. One day, at the age of 16, he was sitting in the courtyard of their home with his mother when Syphus, the local moneylender, came to pay them a visit. Syphus was a very greedy man. He loaned money and assets to the peasants, using their land as collateral. He charged these poor people exorbitant interest on all the monies that he lent. If anyone became indebted to him, they were never able to buy their way out from his claws and tentacles. Ever since Hector's father died, Syphus had his eye on Angela. Hector was too young to understand all that. Poor Angela, who was heartbroken by the loss of her husband, suffered abuse and torments from Syphus, who wanted her to become his mistress. On this occasion, just as she had done for a long time, Angela resisted him with all her strength and forbearance. Hector and his family were indebted to Syphus as a result of the borrowings they had made during the draught that came immediately after the death of Hector's father. The family had worked hard to pay back Syphus, but never had enough to completely pay back all the money they had borrowed.

Once again, a few weeks later, Syphus came to their house to collect his dues. Hector had been behind with his payment as their crops had failed that year. Syphus was drunk and abusive. He demanded immediate payment from Angela or else he would repossess their land and drive the family out of their home. Poor Angela pleaded with the ruthless man for more time, but he would not listen. Hector tried to interject, but Syphus immediately drowned his protests by shouting and screaming at the top of his voice. After a tirade that lasted more than three hours, Syphus agreed to leave them alone, if and only if, Angela would go to his mansion and spend a few days with him. The poor woman had no option but to succumb. Hector was in floods of tears as he could not do much to help. After all, he only knew about farming and selling crops in the market. There had not been a male figure in his life to guide him on important matters and to teach him to fight like the rest of his friends. Angela left with Syphus, never to return again. Hector desperately tried to find his mother, with no success. He was not allowed to get past the gates of Syphus's mansion as he sought his beloved mother. Hector was now left all alone to care for his family's farm and house.

One day, some seven years later, as he sat on a rock at the entrance of his farm, he saw a white horse approaching him. The rider was dressed in armour and held a long, glistening sword in his hand. Hector had not seen this man before. He was obviously a warrior, but he was not Roman. He had dark skin and hazel-brown eyes. Hector walked over to the horseman, greeted him and offered him a drink of water. The horseman accepted and sat down with Hector. He introduced himself as Abbas, the knight of the Kingdom of Abyssinia. He spoke softly and gently, which was in contrast to his strong, hard, powerful appearance. Abbas explained to Hector that he was on his way with a group of soldiers to deliver a message from the king of Abyssinia to the Emperor Marcus of Rome. On the way, some Roman soldiers attacked his entourage and forbade him to travel any further towards the royal palace of the emperor. Abbas fought and killed all the Roman soldiers in the battle. However, he sadly lost all his men in the process. Abbas told his entire story to Hector, who listened intently.

Hector then shared his own sad story with Abbas, who was overcome with grief for this poor boy. Hector invited Abbas to spend a few days with him at his home before proceeding with his journey. Abbas agreed. He still had the message to deliver to the emperor, but he was now alone and needed help to get past all the soldiers and into the royal palace. The relationship between Rome and Abyssinia was not cordial. Abbas was determined to fulfil his mission since the king had chosen him as a trusted emissary to deliver the very important message to the emperor, no matter what obstacles lay before him. He appreciated Hector's kindness and the opportunity to rest, and plan the rest of his journey.

In the coming few weeks, Hector and Abbas became very close friends. Hector looked upon Abbas as a mentor who taught him how to fight cleverly and strategically. He taught Hector about the Abyssinian ways of dealing with enemies, war and self-protection. Hector had a natural talent when it came to combat. He just didn't know that he had this ability. In a very short time, Hector became a first-class fighter, planner and strategist. Abbas took great pains to train Hector well. During this period, Abbas also made two failed attempts to deliver his king's message to the emperor.

One morning, Abbas and Hector set out once again towards the royal palace. They disguised themselves as monks and entered the gates of the palace on the back of an ox-cart. Through ingenious, well-planned steps, they made their way towards the emperor's courtyard. They took a route that led them through the chambers of the maidens, who served the emperor as his mistresses. The empress kept a tight reign over the maidens, who had been instructed to obey her rules in the presence of the emperor. With their faces almost covered, Abbas and Hector walked into the maidens' chambers. Their plan was to enter the courtyard once the emperor had arrived and called his court into session. As they walked through the chambers, they saw the empress coming towards them with the Royal Princess Claudia by her side. Abbas and Hector remained calm as the royal ladies approached. The empress asked Abbas, "Father, what brings you to our chambers?"

Abbas, who was not prepared for this encounter, did some quick thinking and calmly replied, "Your Majesty, we were summoned to come to the chambers to help one of the maidens who is ill and is in need of healing. We are here to pray for her."

This was their lucky day, as indeed, there was a sick maiden in the chambers and the empress believed that the monks had come to pray for her. The princess kept looking at Hector throughout the conversation. When their eyes met, they were both mesmerised. Claudia felt her heart pounding, and so did Hector! He had never felt this way before. The way the princess looked at him moved something in the middle of his chest, and caused him to feel a lump building up in his throat. He was speechless. He too had touched her heart in the same way. The empress directed the two monks towards the private bedroom where the ill maiden lay. The princess asked her mother, "May I go and pray for the maiden with these clergymen?"

The empress was surprised at this request, as she had never known the princess to take an interest in any of the maidens. She paused for a moment and then said, "Of course, my dear Claudia."

The princess walked with Abbas and Hector to the private bedroom of the sick maiden. The empress went a separate way to her chambers. Once in the bedroom, Abbas pretended to pray, while the princess continued to look at Hector with love and tenderness in her eyes. She came close to him and lowered the robe that covered his face. She wanted to look at this handsome man, the son of a peasant. It was love at first sight. Somehow, Princess Claudia knew that Hector was not a monk. She also realised that Abbas, who had revealed his dark skin accidentally, was not a monk either. Rather than expose them, she asked Hector what the reason for his visit to the palace was. Unable to lie to this beautiful woman, who had captured his heart, he revealed to her that he was a peasant from the northern hills who had come to help his friend deliver a message from the king of Abyssinia to her father. She offered to help, but being a curious girl, Claudia asked Abbas, "What is this message that you wish to deliver to my father?"

Abbas replied, "My lady, I have no knowledge of what is contained in the pouch. This is a message of utmost secrecy from my king and this is why he chose me to personally deliver it to your father. In doing so, it is possible that I may never leave this palace again alive."

The Princess, who had a compassionate heart, said to Abbas, "I will help you, and I promise you will leave this palace alive."

They heard the sound of the trumpets, which announced the arrival of the emperor in his court. The princess suggested that Hector remain in the maiden's bedroom and that Abbas cover his face and walk with her as if he was accompanying her.

The plan worked, and Abbas walked with the princess into the emperor's court. She walked up to her father and took a seat next to him, which was usually reserved for her mother. Abbas stood before the emperor and bowed. He then lowered his face-cover. There was a sudden silence in the court. What was this dark Abyssinian doing before the great emperor? The Emperor Marcus, who was surprised by this sudden, uninvited appearance, exclaimed, "By what authority do you present yourself before me? Guards, arrest him!"

Abbas quickly spoke, "Your Majesty, I bring to you an urgent, secret message from my king."

Before the soldiers could seize him, he quickly handed the lion-skin pouch that contained the message to the emperor. The emperor accepted it. He sat back on his throne and opened the pouch. By this time, the soldiers had seized Abbas and dragged him out of the court. The princess watched this event with sadness. Her father was a very harsh man, and dark-skinned people were never allowed to come anywhere near him. The emperor read the message quickly. His face turned grim. The king of Abyssinia had sent the note to warn the great emperor that his most trusted General Tyrus was planning to overthrow the emperor and seize power. Tyrus had led many attacks against the Abyssinians, and everyone feared him for his ruthlessness and cruelty. The last thing anybody wanted was for Tyrus to become the emperor of Rome! The king of Abyssinia had learned of the plot to overthrow the emperor and felt that sending the message of caution would help mend relations with Rome and preserve peace in the region.

The last sentence in the king's message to the emperor read, "I send you this message through the hands of my most trusted knight, Abbas, and beg you to keep this message a complete secret, as you may be surrounded by supporters of Tyrus. You cannot trust anyone."

The emperor heeded the warning and remained silent. He instructed his soldiers to imprison Abbas so as not to give rise to any suspicion with his counsellors that Abbas had delivered to him an important warning.

The Princess left the court to join Hector in the maiden's bedroom. She had fallen in love with this handsome, young peasant. All she wanted to do was to be with him for every moment of her life. She told Hector about what had happened and cautioned him not to try to do anything to rescue Abbas. She promised to keep an eye on Abbas and to inform Hector as soon as she found out what her father's intentions were. In the middle of the night, she arranged to have Hector escorted out of the palace gates. Hector and Claudia had fallen deeply in love with one another. All this had happened in one short day!

In the coming days, she visited Hector regularly with the help of her trusted nurse, Nadina, who had looked after her since she was a baby. Claudia knew that she could no longer live without Hector. But, how could she possibly announce this to anyone in the palace other than to Nadina?

In the meantime, Emperor Marcus took steps to consolidate his power. But it was too late. Tyrus carried out his attack against the emperor and overthrew him from the throne. Now, Rome had a new emperor, Tyrus!

Claudia's father was slain, and she was put into prison together with her mother. All Hector could do was to try and learn whatever little he could about what was happening in the palace. Claudia no longer came to see him. Abbas was also still in jail. The soldiers of Rome had turned very harshly against all the local citizens. This was a new era of tyranny!

Hector practiced his fighting skills daily. He knew that one day very soon, he would have to do something to rescue his beloved Claudia, and his friend and mentor, Abbas. His heart ached for his mother also, as he wondered if she was still alive.

Then, one day, Hector learned of an announcement from the palace that the great gladiator Lance had asked the emperor for the hand of Claudia in marriage. Lance was one of Tyrus's favourite warriors, having dutifully fought by his side in every battle. Tyrus had consented to Lance's request and the news of the marriage spread across the Roman Empire like wildfire. Everyone feared Lance. He had never lost a battle to anyone.

The news of the wedding filled Hector's heart with rage. Later, when he had calmed down, he remembered the words of his friend Abbas, "Always guard against anger, hatred, jealousy, revenge and fear, for they are the ingredients of defeat. Be calm and think through all your options carefully and cleverly. Approach every battle with no emotion, just precision. With this approach, you can never lose." Hector dressed up as a monk again and went back into the palace. Like his friend Abbas had done before, he made his way into the court of Tyrus as a clergyman. He sought permission to speak to the emperor and his request was granted. Tyrus was a very curious and paranoid man who always needed to know everything.

Hector plucked up courage and said to the Emperor Tyrus, "Your Majesty, I have heard of the proposed marriage of Princess Claudia to the Gladiator Lance. I beg to contest this marriage with a challenge to Lance — a duel in the Great Coliseum. May the winner of the duel have the hand of the beautiful Claudia. This is my prayer."

The Emperor Tyrus was highly amused by the monk, who dared to challenge his best warrior. In keeping with his code of honour, he replied, "Your prayer is granted. Your challenge is accepted. Furthermore, I caution you that you will not survive against Lance for more than a minute!"

Hector calmly replied, "Your Majesty, what if I do survive for more than a minute?"

The vain Tyrus laughed and replied, "I will grant you anything you wish for! Of course, you won't be alive to make your wish!"

Everyone in the court burst out laughing. Hector remained calm and silent. The Emperor Tyrus set the time for the duel. He was most amused with everything he had seen and heard!

At the appointed hour, Hector and Lance appeared in the Great Coliseum before Emperor Tyrus and Empress Liana. The crowd became silent as the emperor stood up to speak.

He announced to the people of Rome, "We gather here today to witness the combat between the Great Lance, a warrior who has brought fame and victory to our land, and Hector, the son of a peasant who has challenged the Great Lance to this duel. The prize of this combat is Claudia, daughter of Marcus, a man who was too weak to rule Rome with the power and dignity that Rome commands from the world."

With a smirk on his face, the emperor continued, "Oh yes, one more thing. I have agreed to grant Hector anything he wishes if he survives this battle for more than a minute, providing of course, he is alive to make that wish!"

The crowd burst into laughter. The emperor looked at his empress with a smile on his face.

Hector came forward and said, "Your Majesty, may I have permission to address thee and my fellow Romans who have gathered here?"

The emperor replied, "Permission granted! Speak, for these may be your last words."

Hector then said, "O Great Emperor and the people of Rome. I engage in this combat in the name of love and friendship. I have loved Princess Claudia from the very first moment I set eyes on her. She means everything in the world to me. I also engage in this duel for my friend Abbas, who sits in jail today. This man is my friend, brother, mentor, and everything to me. If fighting Lance here today is the only way for me to win the love of my life and to free my dearest friend, then I accept this combat with everything that I possess in my heart and soul. In their names, I lay down my life and everything that is me. I have nothing against my competitor, the Great Lance. However, to win my love and my friend, this competition must be."

With these words, Hector stepped back and pulled out his sword. He was going to use Abbas' sword to fight Lance.

The amused emperor looked at Lance and said, "Since our peasant here has had his chance to speak, what do you wish to say in response?"

The Great Lance stepped forward, bowed to the emperor and then said, "I am the Great Lance, whose name alone causes people to tremble. I have fought more wars than I can count, and never has anyone dared to challenge me. Whatever I want, I take. I am here to teach all a lesson today, never ever to challenge the Great Lance. I will slay this peasant before your eyes and take the woman I want. This is Lance's word to you."

With the pride and arrogance of a thousand peacocks, Lance stepped back and drew his sword.

The emperor proclaimed, "May the combat begin!"

Lance rushed to attack Hector with all his brute force. Hector was an unknown entity in his eyes, a mere peasant who he could slay in his sleep! He swung his sword at Hector with over-confidence. Hector stepped aside in self-defence. He remembered Abbas's words, "Fight cleverly and strategically.

Have no emotions, just precision. Use your enemy's weakness to your advantage. Arrogance, pride and over-confidence are the greatest weaknesses of all, which you must exploit and sever."

What followed was a fierce combat. After one minute had passed, the emperor shouted, "Stop!"

The gladiators obeyed. The emperor said to Hector, "You have survived one minute! Name your wish."

Hector replied, "Your Majesty, I pray that my friend Abbas be released from prison and be allowed to go back to his home."

The emperor laughed and said, "Your wish will be granted if you survive this combat! If this man is your friend and mentor, let us humour him by bringing him here to watch his pupil slain by the Great Lance."

The crowd cheered. In a few minutes, Abbas was brought to the Coliseum to witness the combat. Hector was thrilled to see his dear friend again. Abbas smiled calmly at him, as if saying, "Let's not rejoice yet, the battle is not over."

Once again, Lance charged at Hector with huge swings of his long, cold sword. Hector dodged smartly. He watched Lance's moves carefully, just as Abbas had taught him. Lance took long, wide strokes and never bothered to defend himself, as he did not expect Hector to be able to strike at him.

Hector remembered Abbas' words, "Be calm and look deep into the eyes of the enemy. Look into his soul and strike with all your might as he exposes his weakest points to you."

Hector methodically followed this advice, and as his piercing eyes met Lance's, there was a brief pause. No one had ever looked into Lance's eyes and his soul like that before. In that brief pause, Hector struck and drove his sword right into Lance's exposed chest, delivering a deadly blow. Lance collapsed in a pool of blood. His eyes were filled with pain and disbelief. He tried to move but couldn't. Hector did not strike again, even though the rules of the combat required him to slay the opponent, Lance. Hector dropped his sword and bowed to the emperor, who by now had stood up in shock. The Great Lance had fallen, but was not dead as yet.

Hector stepped forward and said, "Your Majesty, I pray for permission to spare the life of Lance, for I have no quarrel with him."

The emperor replied, "Permission granted."

Hector looked at Abbas, who smiled at him with approval. He had instilled in Hector the words of wisdom from Abyssinia, which said, "Life is precious. If you cannot give life, then you have no right to take life."

Strangely enough, these were the same words that his mother, Angela, had repeatedly said to him. One day, as Hector chopped down a tree in the farm for fun, his mother said to him, "He who cannot give life has no right to take life."

The combat was over. The emperor released Abbas and allowed Hector to marry the love of his life. The emperor offered Hector the position of general, even though Hector disapproved of wars and hated killing anything. As Hector considered turning down the offer, Abbas said to him, "Accept the position. This is your chance to change things for the better. Show them what you have learnt about life and compassion. Change others by your thoughts and examples."

A few days later, the emperor summoned Hector in his presence and said, "Hector, you put your life at risk in that competition. Were your friend and Claudia truly worth that price?"

Hector smiled and replied, "If there had been a peaceful way for me to win my friend and my bride, I would have chosen that path. I would not have engaged in the combat. However, that was the only avenue available to me. Therefore, I did not think about the price that had to be paid. I thought about the love and friendship that was to be gained. It is with that spirit that I fought the Great Lance."

The emperor shook his head and said, "This is truly amazing. One gladiator engages in a competition because of his pride, arrogance and anger at having been challenged by a lesser opponent and the other engages in the competition to gain love and friendship. There is much to be learned about competitions and why people enter into them. What really is success and what really is defeat?"

Hector replied, "Even if I had lost my life in the competition, it would have been success for me, because my *motive* was to gain love and friendship. This, I could have achieved in life or in death."

The emperor, who was astounded with what he had just heard asked, "Hector, where did you learn to think like this?"

Hector replied, "Your Majesty, I lost my father when I was only eight years old. My mother raised me to be a farmer, and a good farmer is all I wanted to be. She taught me about the life that came from the seeds that I planted. The seeds grew into plants, which, in turn, bore the fruits that I harvested. She taught me to respect life and to respect nature. I learned to look at my plants and to look at people in the same way, because we all are part of life itself. "In life," my mother always said, "There is no success or failure, because life is a journey, not a destination.""

The Emperor Tyrus, who himself was a great warrior, was touched by the words of this simple peasant. He inquired, "Where is this great lady who raised such a special child?"

With tears in his eyes, Hector relayed to the emperor the story of his mother and how he had lost her to Syphus. The emperor immediately sent his soldiers to arrest Syphus and bring him before the court to answer for his actions. Only a day earlier, Emperor Tyrus would have thought nothing about usury, exploitation of the poor and abuse of women. Yet, here he was today, touched in his soul by the son of a peasant.

That afternoon, as the court was in session, Syphus was brought in chains, shaking with fear, before the emperor and Hector. Syphus fell to his knees and begged for forgiveness.

"Where is Angela, the mother of Hector?" the emperor demanded to know.

In a shaking voice Syphus replied, "She is no longer alive your majesty. She died many years ago at my home."

The emperor stood up and shouted, "You are not only a wretched coward, you are a murderer too! You will pay for this with your life!"

Hector was overcome with grief at the news of his mother's death. He knew that she would have died a painful death at the hands of this horrible man.

With tears in his eyes he said, "Your Majesty, when this man took my mother away, I lay awake for many nights thinking about how I could take revenge for what he had done. My heart and my mind were filled with hatred, anger and thirst for his blood! But, as I looked at the plants in the field, bearing their fruits each season, I realised that this is not what my mother would have wanted me to feel or think about. She always taught me that hatred and revenge were forces of destruction, which should have no room in my life. I was a farmer, a gardener, someone who was the sower of seeds and the caretaker of life. I was to be life itself, she always said. Your Majesty, I beg you to spare this man's life. In exchange for his life, he must give back all the land that he has extorted from the poor peasants. He must give back life and livelihood to all those little Hectors out there who have suffered at his hands."

The emperor replied, "Hector, your wish is granted. I always thought that revenge was sweet. But, from you I have learnt that life itself is sweeter!"

Hector served the emperor for the rest of his life. He and Claudia were blessed with lovely children. Abbas returned to Abyssinia. Hector and Abbas became the architects of peace that followed between the two nations.

There are many lessons that we can learn from the story of Hector. There are numerous examples in it of *positive* and *negative motivations*. For example, some of the *negative motivations* include Syphus' greed, which caused him to exploit the poor peasants; his lust for Angela that caused him to torment her family and take her away to her death; the Emperor Marcus' prejudice towards dark-skinned people; Tyrus' lust for power that led him to overthrow Marcus; Tyrus' vanity and scorn that caused him to belittle Hector; Lance's arrogance and condescending attitude that *motivated* him to enter into the combat with the sole purpose of showing that he was the greatest; etc.

There are also numerous examples of *positive motivations*, some of which include Hector's desire to be a good farmer; the care that he took of his family; the warmth and generosity that he showed towards Abbas; Abbas' determination to fulfil the command and trust of his king; the princess' kindness towards Abbas in helping him fulfil his mission; the love that existed between Hector and Claudia; Abbas' desire to train Hector to become a warrior so that he could fight and defend himself; Hector's challenge to fight Lance in order to free Abbas and Claudia; Hector's compassion in not slaying Lance; Hector's acceptance of the position of general so that he could positively influence others with his ideals; Hector's love and respect for life; his ability to overcome the desire for revenge against Syphus even though he could have executed Syphus, the man who caused him so much pain; Abbas and Hector's efforts to bring peace between Rome and Abyssinia; etc.

Positive and *negative motivations* influence all our actions, feelings and attitudes. *Positive motivations* have the tendency to reduce or eliminate conflict. *Negative motivations* cause us to unleash negative energies that can lead to destruction and pain to ourselves and to those around us. *Negative motivations* fuel conflict and spread unhappiness. Therefore, we should think about, analyse and understand our *motivations* carefully.

When we feel anger or frustration, we need to stop and look at the *motivations* that are driving the events that are causing this anger and frustration. If we can identify the *negative motivations*, we can take steps to overcome them and replace them with *positive motivations*. It is very healthy to ask the question, "Why am I doing this?" or, "Why do I feel this way about things?" Simply asking such questions leads us a long way towards the answer.

When we analyse the concept of competition carefully, we will recognise that our entire life is surrounded by competition. Competition can be healthy, or it can be very destructive. It depends entirely upon the *motivation* with which we enter into the competition. Hector's *motivation* was love and friendship. Lance's *motivation* was vanity and arrogance. Lance ended up paying the price for his negative attitude. We can extrapolate the story and events surrounding Hector's life into our own daily lives. We may be living under different sets of circumstances today, but our feelings, attitudes and actions are still driven by similar *motivations*. We should carefully guard against *motivations* that are driven by anger, greed, hatred, revenge, jealousy, pride, arrogance and other negative traits. These traits should not be allowed to exist within our minds and our being, for they are sources of pain and conflict. Instead, we should think about harnessing within ourselves traits of love, compassion, care, forgiveness, generosity, fairness, respect and other similar qualities. These qualities bring about positive feelings, which reduce, and sometimes eliminate, conflict.

Angela taught her son Hector a very important lesson. "Life is not a competition between success and failure. Life is experience. Life is worthy of our utmost respect." If we think about our attitudes and feelings from such a perspective, we will be able to view our challenges and circumstances more objectively. We will then be able to approach life from a position of clarity, strength and peace. We will be able to achieve a healthy sense of *neutrality* within ourselves. This will take us one step closer *towards zero conflict.*

In order to practise identifying *positive* and *negative motivations,* I suggest that you re-read the story of Hector and Lance once again, and list all the *positive motivations* and all the *negative motivations* that you can find. Record your feelings as you go through each of the *motivations* in the story. Then, reflect upon your greatest successes and failures in life and try to identify the *motivations* that lay behind the events that led you to these climactic experiences. The process of identifying and understanding *motivations* is a valuable tool in evaluating the fundamental driving forces behind all our daily actions.

Seeds of Resolution

❋ Let us contemplate and internalise the following seed of empowerment:

"MAY MY MOTIVATIONS BE POSITIVE AND PURE..."

❋ These words possess an energy that will permeate through all our thoughts and actions. They will add purity to the purpose behind everything that we do.

❋ At the end of each day, we should reflect upon the one thing, event or experience that brought us the greatest happiness during the day. We should identify the *motivations* that led us to this experience.

❋ Then, we should reflect upon the one thing, event or experience that caused us the greatest frustration, hurt or disappointment. Once again, we should identify the *motivations* that led us to this experience.

❋ When we experience conflicts during the day, we should ask ourselves questions such as,

What are the motivations behind this conflict?
Why am I facing this situation?
What can I do to change things?
Do I need to be in this situation at all?

❋ When we become aware of our *motivations* and the *motivations* of others, we will be in a better position to build successful relationships, achieve our goals in life, and find peace and happiness. This is the path *towards zero conflict.*

134

My Reflections

Now   date: / /   .

My Reflections

One Year Hence   date: / / .

Chapter 9

FEAR

*"Embrace that which you fear
and you will have power over it."*

In Chapter 8, we discussed motivations *and their impact on our lives.* Fear *is a very important* negative motivation, *which deserves a chapter of its own.*

What is fear? *Where does it come from? Where does it reside? What does it do to us? As we ponder these questions, the following answers come to mind:*

Fear *is a powerful* motivation, *which causes us to act in a manner that often defies reason and good judgment. It is a force of repulsion that creates anxiety, pain, frustration and unhappiness.*

Fear *is an illusion that resides only in the future. It uses the future as its weapon to destroy the present.*

Fear *comes from our inability to embrace the unknown. It reigns in the absence of trust and causes us to be suspicious and paranoid. It is an illusion that resides in the mind, which makes it both powerful and weak.*

Fear *is one of the greatest sources of both inner and outer conflict. It is a source of weakness and therefore must be mastered in order to achieve peace, happiness and zero conflict.*

The following story is an excerpt from my second book, Parables from the Origin, *which provides an interesting perspective on* fear *and how it can be overcome:*

THE PARABLE OF THE SLAVE

One dark, starry night, King Marcus sat with his philosopher, Juan, in the gardens of the royal palace, talking about a case that the king had to judge the next day. By nature, King Marcus was paranoid. He trusted no one and assumed the worst in every situation. As a result, he waged many wars against his neighbours, as well as in kingdoms that were too far away to cause him any harm. His military advisors deviously took advantage of his paranoia by instigating rumours of his neighbours' hostile intentions. In this way, they could personally benefit from the looting and plundering that usually accompanied the attacks. King Marcus was now 50 years old, and he was the most powerful king in the region. He had no friends and preferred to be alone most of the time.

On this particular evening, he was seeking the counsel of Juan on the case of Azam, the slave, who had bought his freedom through hard work, and had subsequently established himself as a successful merchant in the land. Azam's competitors had plotted to destroy his enterprise and discredit him to the point where he could be enslaved again. They had set up a trade with Azam: six sacks of his good rice in exchange for six gold coins. Poor, unsuspecting Azam delivered his rice and collected the six coins. He was not aware that his enemies had replaced the good sacks of rice in his store with very poor quality rice, which was not even fit to be fed to the chickens! There were many witnesses to the transaction.

As Azam was walking back to his home, he was arrested by the king's soldiers and charged with fraud and theft. He was immediately imprisoned, awaiting trial. Azam's enemies arranged to have his case heard by the king himself, because they wanted to set an example to all the slaves who sought freedom. The king did not know anything about this.

The king asked Juan, "Tell me about the slave Azam. Where is he from and why is he being charged with fraud and theft?"

Juan replied, "Azam was brought to our land by the Arab traders. I believe he is from West Africa. The slave traders picked him up in his village ten years ago, when he was thirteen years old. Isaac, the corn miller, bought him from the traders. Isaac is an unusual man. He told Azam that he could earn his freedom if he milled a thousand sacks of corn every year for seven years."

Marcus interjected, "That is impossible! No man could mill a thousand sacks per year!"

"That is indeed correct," Juan replied. "But young Azam was so determined to become a free man that he worked without stopping for the full seven years. He hardly slept during the night, and toiled throughout the day. At the end of the seven years, Isaac kept his word and freed Azam. This caused the people in the kingdom to become very upset because, as Your Majesty is well aware, it is unusual in our land for slaves to earn their freedom and be allowed to live as equal citizens. To make matters worse, Azam decided to become a rice trader. To everyone's surprise, he began to prosper more than his competitors. Of course, now we can see a possible reason for his success. He probably profited by selling poor-quality rice at prices that deserved much better quality."

"That is despicable!" King Marcus said. "If he did that, he should pay for it! But Juan, I ask you, how could a man with such a strong will, get involved in such fraudulent activities? Do you not think that his seven years of hard labour would have taught him to keep out of trouble? If he bought his freedom at such a high price, do you not think this man understands the concept of value? There is something here that does not meet the eye."

"Yes, it does seem strange," Juan replied, "but he was caught red-handed. There were many witnesses!"

King Marcus then asked, "How should I judge him tomorrow?"

"You will need to know the truth before you can judge him," Juan replied. "Even though he was caught red-handed, there may be certain facts that remain unknown. Until you know the unknown, how can you judge him?"

King Marcus was confused by this statement. He asked the philosopher, "How can there be an unknown? The facts are quite clear. All I need to do now is pass judgment. This is what I do in all situations. I decide what the truth is and I act accordingly. I do not like to waste time."

Juan replied, "At the risk of offending you, my Great King, I must disagree. How many times have you declared war on our neighbours when you simply *thought* that their intentions were hostile? You did not know for sure what their intentions were. You may recall that in the past 30 battles, you were the one who attacked first 29 times! If the truth as you perceived it were correct, we would have been attacked more than once!"

King Marcus did not like what he was hearing. "Our neighbours could not be trusted!" he shouted. "They were always plotting against me. I had to destroy them!"

Juan, who knew his position was precarious, said, "That is true, O Beloved King. But how about the other 20 battles you waged against kingdoms that were too far away to affect us?"

The king replied, "I heard of their intentions through my informants. They posed a threat, so I had to attack!"

"How do you know that your informants were telling the truth?" Juan asked. "From what I know, we have waged wars against peaceful people for a long time now. I believe that you attacked them because of what you did not know, rather than what you had heard. Surely you must have wondered what the truth really was."

"To me they represented the unknown," the king replied. "I did not trust any of them. Therefore, I had to attack them lest they decided to attack me. Believe me, Juan, when I say that I do not enjoy war. The battlefield terrifies me! But I have to do what is necessary."

"You attacked everyone out of *fear*, O Beloved King," Juan then said. "You could not accept the unknown and this fuelled your *fear*. Even in the battlefield you fought out of *fear* because you knew not what would happen next!"

Marcus was furious. He shouted, "Juan, you could pay for this insolence with your life! How dare you call me a coward?"

Poor Juan, now shaken, replied, "I am sorry if I have offended you, my Great King. I did not intend to suggest that you were a coward. I see a great difference between *fear* and cowardice. *Fear* exists in all of us. It causes us to attack or to run. He that runs is a coward. You, my Great King, are not a coward. This I can attest to with my life!"

The king was soothed by this remark. "Juan, I cannot deny that I feel *fear* in everything I do. It is with me all the time," he said. "When I do not know what lies ahead, *fear* dominates me. But I also have great courage, for I have no hesitation in facing my enemy. And Juan, you know well that I have a great number of enemies who would do anything to bring my kingdom down."

The philosopher replied, "Yes, O Great King, you are so right. I too lived in *fear* until one day I realised that every moment of my life that lay ahead of me was an unknown. I learned to accept the unknown. Since then I have not felt the pains of *fear*. In a strange way, by accepting the unknown, I learned to *trust* and this gave me a completely different outlook towards myself, my neighbours and everyone I encountered. I was not suspicious of anyone any more and that made people feel more at ease being with me. You see, O Great King, I do not believe that you have as many enemies as you think you have. *Fear* creates enemies in our minds. As long as we *fear*, our enemies exist. As soon as we stop *fearing*, they disappear!"

"You are right, Juan," King Marcus observed. "All my life I have found great difficulty in dealing with the unknown. Through my *fear* I have destroyed a great deal. I have banished people from the kingdom because I wrongly suspected their intentions. Each time I speak to my military advisors, I feel my heart pounding against my chest as I hear about more new enemies. Each time I go to battle, my stomach churns with *fear* of losing or being killed. It is a horrible feeling, Juan, as I am sure you know. The fact that you have the courage to be so frank with me tells me that you have no *fear*. I can learn a great deal from you."

"O Great King, our religion teaches us to have faith," Juan commented, "and we often wonder what that means. Behind all our elaborate rituals, lies the simple concept of belief. This belief can be in God, nature, our friends, loved ones, or anything for that matter. But to believe in something requires one to embrace the unknown. *Fear* comes from our inability to embrace the unknown."

King Marcus had learnt much from the philosopher that evening. The next morning, Juan joined him at the trial of the slave. The court was filled with spectators. King Marcus was surprised with the size of the turnout at this trial. It made him curious. After the charges had been read to Azam, the king asked him, "Young Azam, what do you wish to say in your defence to these grave charges?"

The slave replied, "O Mighty King Marcus, I am innocent. I have committed no fraud. The night before the transaction, my store was filled with rice of the best quality. When I did the trade for the six gold coins, I genuinely believed that I had delivered the best of my produce. I was astonished to find that the sacks contained poor quality rice. They must have been switched. You can ask the people from whom I purchase my rice. They will attest to the fact that I only buy the best of their produce. This is why I have enjoyed success in my trading."

"Are you suggesting that someone stole your good rice and replaced it with the inferior produce that you traded that day?" the king asked, in a raised voice. "This is a very serious allegation that you make, Azam!"

The slave replied, "Your Majesty, I cannot say for sure what happened, as I was not present to witness the change of the sacks. Therefore, I cannot explain how it happened. But what I do know for sure is that I did not buy, nor did I own, the inferior-quality rice."

"I have heard about how you bought your freedom through hard work," the king remarked. "Surely during the seven years that you toiled for Isaac, you never really knew that he would indeed keep his word, did you?"

Azam replied, "No, Your Majesty, I did not. But I *trusted* him to keep his word."

The king then asked, "How could you have placed seven years of your life in Isaac's hands purely on *trust*? Where did you learn to *trust* like that?"

The slave replied, "Your Majesty, one day, when I was thirteen years old, I was playing with my father outside our hut as my mother and sisters watched. We were a happy family. Then from behind the bushes appeared the slave catchers, with their daggers and ropes. As they tried to catch me, my father came to my rescue and one of the ruthless catchers stuck a dagger in his heart. I rushed to hold my dying father's head in my arms, but I was torn away by the strong hands of my captors. My mother and sisters were also taken away as slaves, and I have not seen them since. Your Majesty, in one brief moment, my entire world came to an end. The morning before I was captured, I had no idea of the terrible things that would happen to me in a few hours. And, after I was captured, I did not know where I was going to be taken or what I was going to do. I was terrified. Each time a leaf moved in the wind, my heart stopped with *fear*! But, in time, I learned to accept that whatever lay ahead of me was a journey that would shape my life. This journey was full of unknowns. As I thought about it, I realised that my entire life was an unknown from the moment that I was born. When I finally learned to embrace the unknown, I was no longer afraid. I learned to trust and have faith in God, and this helped me to overcome my *fear*. Your Majesty, I am completely alone in this world, and therefore, I have learned to be my own best friend. I have learned to *trust* myself and this has helped me to *trust* others. This is why I was able to *trust* Isaac's word so freely."

King Marcus was dumbfounded with the story of the slave. "Azam, you are a remarkable man!" he said. "For a person who has suffered such disruptions and violence in his life, I would have thought that every moment of your day and night would be filled with *fear*. Yet here you are, calm and confident, sharing with us all the strength of your *trust*. You must truly have great faith in God and yourself. A man like you is too solid in character to commit the fraud for which you have been accused! I therefore pronounce you a free man!"

With his eyes filled with tears, Azam said to the king, "Your Majesty, I am truly grateful to you for granting me my freedom. May God bless you."

"Young Azam, I am truly grateful to you," the king replied, "for you have taught me how to free myself from my *fears!* In some special way, you have brought peace to our land, because I will not attack our neighbours again, simply out of my *fear.* Our kingdom owes you much, Azam. Go in peace and may God bless you too." King Marcus then looked at Juan, and smiled. Juan smiled back.

"O Great King Marcus," Juan began, "no philosopher could ever explain so beautifully the special place that faith, *trust* and hope should hold in our hearts. Fate dealt the harshest of cards to Azam. Yet, look where the strength of his faith has brought him. Behold, my Great King, we have much to correct!"

Fear lives in the future. It embeds itself in our minds like a virus and causes us to anticipate negative events. However, as we have learnt from the story of Azam, if we embrace the unknown, we will have power over our *fears.*

We can also overcome *fear* by bringing the future events that we dread into the present. This is illustrated in the following two stories:

THE DYING SON

Richard was a 40-year-old father, who paced up and down the hospital corridor while his 16-year-old son, Timothy, lay dying in an intensive care unit. Timothy had only been given two hours to live. Richard *feared* the moment when the doctor would tell him that his beloved son had passed away. Richard spent the next two hours pacing the corridor, in pure *fear*, until the inevitable happened. He had lost, forever, the last two precious hours of Timothy's life wrapped up in *fear*. Instead of pacing the corridors, he could have talked to his son, from the heart, and listened to all the things that Timothy had wanted to say to him. This would probably have been the most important and precious conversation of their lives.

After the funeral, as Richard stood at the grave of his son, he begged forgiveness for all the turmoil that he had caused in his son's life. He yearned to hear his son say, "I forgive you dad, and I will love you forever." Sadly, Richard could have heard these words from his son during the last two hours at the hospital. What a wasted opportunity!

If Richard had learnt what we all know now, he could have brought the future into the present by saying to himself, "Timothy is gone. I accept that he is gone."

In this way, he would have been able to achieve an acceptance of that which he *feared* the most. Overcoming this *fear* would have allowed him to spend quality time with Timothy during the last two precious hours of his life. Those hours would have been priceless!

THE VICTIM OF EXTORTION

Caroline was a successful, attractive, 35-year-old mother of two wonderful children, who was being blackmailed by Jason, a sleazy extortionist, for having an affair with Alan, her business colleague. She lived each day in terror of the moment when her husband, Terry, would find out about the affair. Jason had taken explicit photographs of Caroline and Alan on a beach in Corfu. He thrived on Caroline's *fear*, and extorted whatever he could get from her, including money, sexual favours and other despicable services. Even though she had stopped the affair with Alan soon after the extortion began, Caroline lived a life of hell for ten years, losing all the happiness and opportunities to grow in her life, both materially and spiritually. She cringed each time the mail arrived, or the telephone rang. She was unable to enjoy the time with her family and the love of her husband and children. Although she was capable of being a nurturing mother, she was unable to give her children the quality of attention that they deserved. Her life became a nightmare, as she *feared* the moment when her family would find out about her secret indiscretions with Alan. The pressure and stress eventually caused her to suffer a fatal cardiac failure at the young age of 45. What a waste of a precious life! After her death, Jason moved on to extort his next set of victims.

———————————

If Caroline had learnt to bring the future event that she *feared* into the present, she would have said to herself, "Terry knows about my affair with Alan. I accept the consequences of my actions." Once she had managed to internalise her acceptance of the dreaded future event, she would have been able to tell her husband about her mistake. She would have been ready to 'let the chips fall wherever they were meant to fall'. Maybe Terry would have forgiven her and given her a second chance. Maybe he would have divorced her. Maybe she would have lived by herself or perhaps she would have married again. Whatever the outcome, she would have been able to "live" her life again. No outcome could have been worse than living in *fear* and dying without accomplishing what she had come in this world to achieve. No outcome could have been worse than living the nightmare that she did.

OVERCOMING FEAR

We can all learn from the painful experiences of Richard and Caroline. We can learn to bring the future events that we *fear* into the present, and gain power over them. In this way, we will not waste the precious moments of our lives, living in *fear* and doing things that do not, in the end, serve us well.

The story of Azam, the slave, teaches us that every moment that lies ahead of us is an unknown. Many of us *fear* failure and worry a great deal about what tomorrow may bring to us. Some of us worry about where our livelihood will come from. Some of us worry about what we may lose, or what we may fail to gain. Such worries take on various forms, which cause us to feel anxious and miserable. When we think about the day we were born, did we *really* know where that first bottle of milk was going to come from? Nothing has changed since then — we have only learned to worry about it! Rather than *fear* the unknown, we should accept and embrace the unknown. In this way, we will become *fearless*. There is an element of *trust* that goes with embracing the future or the unknown. This *trust* can be of a mental or a spiritual nature.

At the mental level, we could say, *"What will be, will be."* In this way, we can enable ourselves to accept and embrace the future.

At the spiritual level, we could say, *"I trust in the Origin. I am not alone. The Origin is with me."* This expression of *trust* in the future comes from our faith, regardless of our religious background. There are some who do not believe in God and they attribute their existence to a "Statistical Coincidence." Such people could place their *trust* in this Statistical Coincidence. Faith is a source of immense strength because it brings *trust* into our hearts, which banishes our fears permanently.

Therefore, by understanding and implementing these methods of conquering *fear*, by bringing the future into the present and by embracing the unknown, we can overcome this greatest *negative motivation* of all.

Like poor Caroline, each one of us has a skeleton or many skeletons that are buried in a closet. These skeletons could range from past events and mistakes, to present situations that cause us difficulty and anxiety. It would be helpful for us to be completely honest with ourselves and to carefully list each and every thing that we *fear*. This is a very important exercise, which will enable a true inner understanding of our life and the events that we are experiencing. Our list will also confirm to us that, while the roots of our fears may be in the past, their consequences always dwell in the future, which has not even happened yet! With this understanding, we can empower ourselves by taking the necessary actions in the present to eliminate our fears from our lives, forever. What a blessed relief that would be!

BEING FEARLESS

When we become *fearless*, we can enjoy true freedom and cherish the wonderful gifts that life brings to us. When we become *fearless*, we can enjoy 'true power',

TOWARDS ZERO CONFLICT

through which we can realise our full potential. When those around us, who thrive on our fears, realise that we are indeed *fearless*, they may leave our lives and move on to seek weaker victims. The following short story exemplifies the powers that come from being *fearless*:

THE FATIMID FORT

The Fatimids were a famous Muslim civilisation who ruled large parts of the Middle East, North Africa and Southern Europe many hundreds of years ago. They were people of strong faith and subscribed to the esoteric form of worship in Islam, which was based upon a personal relationship that exists between each human being and his or her Creator. Much has been written about the Fatimids in history books, some complimentary and some rather critical, depending upon the source and the author of the book. Regardless of how historians perceive them, the Fatimids played a very important role in bringing an enriched culture of freedom and knowledge to the world. The Fatimids had one great asset, which was the fact that they were *fearless*.

One day, a great king from Europe decided to attack and capture one of the Fatimid forts in North Africa. He surrounded the fort with an army of around fifty thousand soldiers. There were no more than a thousand Fatimid soldiers inside the fort. Before launching an attack, the king decided to send one of his emissaries with a message to the Fatimids, seeking their surrender to avoid bloodshed. The sun had almost set as the emissary entered the fort. The sky was brightly lit by the fifty thousand flame torches held by the king's soldiers. It was a sight that could have intimidated

152

anyone, let alone a small army of one thousand soldiers, trapped in a fort!

The emissary said to the commander of the fort, "Surrender your fort to our great king, and you will all be allowed to leave in peace. If you do not do so, then the lights of the torches, that have painted the sky red, speak clearly of our intentions. You are hopelessly outnumbered and stand no chance against our army. Our king, who does not seek to shed your blood, offers you this one chance."

The commander smiled and calmly replied, "Tell your great king that we thank him for his offer. We have no quarrel with your king or his people. We seek to be left alone in peace. But, if we are attacked, we shall fight back. Not only will we defeat your army, but we will travel to your nation to stake our claim as retribution for your king's declaration of war upon us."

The emissary burst out laughing and said, "You have a great deal of nerve to challenge a force that can stampede over you in minutes. Look at your soldiers. You are no more than a thousand in number. Look out there! There are fifty thousand of us with weapons you could never match. What weapons do you have in this fort that you could possibly use to defend yourselves? Most certainly you are being an irresponsible commander by sending these thousand young men to the slaughterhouse!"

The commander, who was still calm and smiling, replied, "We possess the greatest weapon of all. We are *fearless!* Let me show you what I mean."

With those words, the commander summoned one of his soldiers and asked him to stand on a tower at the top of the fort.

He then commanded the soldier to jump off the tower. Without a moment's hesitation, the soldier jumped to his death. The emissary froze with shock.

The commander looked into the eyes of the emissary and said, "Tell your king that we are *fearless*. We are above death. Each one of us is equal to a hundred of his men. If we are attacked, we will fight with the power that your king has never seen before. And, when we descend upon his kingdom, all his might and weapons will be like mere specs of dust, which we shall tread upon as if they never existed!"

Still in shock, the emissary rode back to the king and conveyed the message from the commander. He said to the king, "These people are *fearless*. They possess a power that I have never seen before. Even though we outnumber them, they are not a people we really want to attack for we are dealing with an enemy that is above death itself!"

The king, who was a wise man, chose to heed the words of his emissary. The next morning, when the Fatimid commander looked out at the grounds around the fort, there was no army. The king had left peacefully in the night with his army for they did not wish to engage in a battle with the *fearless* ones...

This story demonstrates a dimension of human power that comes from being *fearless*. This human power takes on many different forms, which serve as positive and enabling forces. The absence of *fear* brings clarity of thought, openness of communication, and an outlook towards life that is filled with courage and strength, which facilitates accomplishment.

Seeds of Resolution

❀ Let us reflect upon our lives and identify the sources and impacts of our *fears*.

❀ Let us learn to embrace the unknown and to become *fearless* by contemplating and internalising the following seeds of resolution:

"I AM FREE.
I AM FEARLESS.
I TRUST IN NOW.
I TRUST IN TOMORROW.
I ACCEPT WITH GRATITUDE
ALL THAT IS TO COME..."

❀ These seeds will help to instil within us confidence in ourselves and in the future.

❀ When we reflect upon our *negative motivations*, we should seek to recognise and understand the role that *fear* may have played.

❀ When we reflect upon our *positive motivations*, we should seek to recognise how and where we have managed to overcome our *fears*.

❀ Each morning, we should look towards the day ahead with confidence, hope, and trust, that whatever experiences we are to be blessed with, may bring us the learning and the fulfilment that we seek.

My Reflections

Now   date: / / .

My Reflections

One Year Hence

date: / / .

My Reflections

Chapter 10

OPPRESSION

*"Oppression is the forced imposition
of the will of one person upon another."*

Oppression is the forced imposition of the will of one person upon another, at an individual or at a collective level. Oppression can manifest in many forms, from the exertion of control and domination in relationships at a personal level, to the forced imposition of ideologies, values and governing rules upon a group of people at a community, national and international level. Oppression stems from a variety of factors including greed, hatred, insecurity and fear. Sometimes, oppression exists in subtle forms, especially when it is driven by good intentions. For example, parents often oppress their children unknowingly in their attempts to do their best for their children. Spouses often do the same to their loved ones out of insecurity. Friends sometimes oppress each other out of fear of hurting one another, especially when sensitive personalities are involved. Therefore, oppression needs to be viewed und understood from a broad perspective.

Whatever its underlying source may be, oppression is a self-perpetuating conflict, which must be recognised and overcome. It is our negative motivations that cause us to oppress and act in a manner that causes pain and anguish to those around us.

There are some who enjoy power and dominance over others. There are others who are only happy if they have everything their own way at all times. And, there are those who thrive on taking control of the property, possessions and the personal will of others. These negative motivations manifest themselves in the form of oppression, which, in turn, fuel the conflicts, that can sometimes leave permanent scars on the oppressed.

Many of us exert oppression without actually being aware of it. We exercise control over our spouses, children, loved ones, friends, colleagues and acquaintances. While such control may stem from the best of intentions, we should pause to consider whether oppression is embedded in our actions. We should think about the impact we may be having upon those who are at the receiving end of our actions. We should always carefully examine and seek to identify the negative motivations that may be causing us to oppress others.

If we are the oppressors, we may wish to start thinking about our motivations and the reasons why they exist in our lives. We should reflect upon the origins of these motivations. Of course, we have to be brutally honest with ourselves if we are to discover the true answers. Once we understand the root causes of our negative motivations, and therefore the reasons for our tendency to oppress, we can then proceed towards mending the broken fences in our lives. This may require patience and humility, which are virtues that are not easily attained. However, the peace and happiness that we will discover through eliminating this powerful conflict is well worth the trouble, for it will mark an important turning point in our lives. We can then bring the harmony into our lives that we deserve. Recognising our negative motivations takes us a long way towards overcoming them.

Oppression is usually accompanied by an injustice, which is made worse by fear of depravation, punishment, abandonment, failure and a whole range of other negative outcomes. This fear breeds pain and conflict within those that are oppressed, to a level where their lives can sometimes be described as a nightmare. None of us has the right to inflict such pain upon others. Yet, we do it all the time, in one form or another, be it subtle or obvious.

For those of us who are oppressed, we need to think about the factors that are causing the oppression that we are suffering. We need to work towards overcoming our fears and taking charge of our lives, by using the lessons described in Chapter 9. We need to try and understand the negative motivations that are driving our oppressors. We need to take measures to bring an end to the oppression, either through action or through dialogue. The latter is a very effective tool that we have at our disposal. It would help us to reflect upon questions like:

> *From what angle is my oppressor coming?*
> *Why is he or she oppressing me?*
> *Am I allowing myself to be oppressed?*
> *Am I fuelling this oppression?*
> *Is my fear playing a part in this oppression? If so, how can I conquer this fear?*
> *How can I change my circumstances?*
> *How can I best reason with my oppressor?*
> *What can I do to change my reaction to his or her behaviour towards me?*

There are numerous questions that we can ask ourselves with respect to the oppression that we may be facing in different aspects of our lives. We should try our level best to overcome being oppressed. However, sometimes, after having explored every possible avenue, we may need to be prepared to walk away from the situation. Of course, there are certain situations that we cannot walk away from. Nevertheless, the very fact that we are mentally prepared to do so, bestows upon us an empowerment over the situation, which can be viewed as a constructive solution in the circumstances.

The following story reveals different dimensions of oppression, from the perspective of the oppressor and the oppressed:

THE CORPORATE RAIDER

It was 3.00 p.m., on a cloudy afternoon in New York's Battery Park Plaza. Malcolm Asher, Chairman & CEO of Asher Microchip Inc., a Fortune 100 company in the field of computer chip technology, sat in the boardroom of his plush headquarters, discussing with his board the acquisition of a Memphis-based competitor, Tennessee Electro-Chip Inc. Malcolm's company was much larger in size than Tennessee Electro-Chip Inc., which was owned by Joe Argus, a self-made entrepreneur. Joe had worked hard to build his company, which started with one employee and grew to 600 employees within a period of five years. Malcolm, on the other hand, built Asher Microchip Inc. on a fast-track basis by going public, raising hundreds of millions of dollars in the stock market, poaching all the top cutthroat executives in the industry and buying out all the competitors who were an irritation to Malcolm in the marketplace. Now the time had come for Malcolm's 10,000-employee company to take over Joe's 600- employee company through a merger process that made Tennessee Electro-Chip Inc. a subsidiary of Asher. Joe had agreed to continue to manage the subsidiary as an employee of Asher.

Malcolm and Joe were very different people. Malcolm was a blue chip, Ivy League kid who went to the best schools and colleges in the USA, and earned a Bachelors degree in Engineering and a Masters degree in Business and Law. He was awarded an honorary Ph.D. for his role in revolutionising the computer chip industry. Malcolm was brought up as a silver-spoon child who had everything he ever wanted. Malcolm spent very little time with his parents, who were always busy travelling around the globe or entertaining their business associates and clients. Malcolm was raised by Samantha, a nurse from Southern Georgia, and, as a result, never really knew what parental love was. He grew up very much on his own. Malcolm developed a great passion for the mighty dollar by watching the way his father pursued the accumulation of wealth. He felt that the green piece of paper had the power to make the world turn, and so his goal in life was to become one of the richest men in the world. Human feelings meant little to Malcolm. The only emotion he cared for was that of the dollar — how it performed in the global currency exchanges, how the Dow Jones behaved, how inflation and interest rates fluctuated, how global markets emerged, grew and declined, and how his own personal fortune fared each day. Malcolm believed that his personal wealth gave him power over all beings.

Joe Argus, on the other hand, had very humble beginnings. He grew up on a farm and became involved in the field of business at the age of 13. Joe was a compassionate man who cared deeply about the feelings of others. He was generous and considerate towards everyone, even during the times when he had little or no money in his pocket. Joe had a passion for inventing things and had developed his knowledge in the computer chip industry through stripping down, innovating and re-building computers in his workshop. He rigorously pursued his passion as an inventor and an innovator, which led him to build a successful company in the industry. He treated each one of his employees like a family member. People worked long hours for him, out of love and respect for this special man, who made every person he met feel as if they were the most important thing in his life. Joe had a beautiful wife, Mary, and two sons, Michael and Sam. Joe was not enthusiastic about selling his company to Malcolm, despite the fact that he was offered a large sum for his company in the form of Asher stock.

Malcolm lived a lifestyle of the rich and famous. He owned a private jet, which took him all over the globe every few weeks. Like his father, he rarely saw his wife, Elena, and daughter, Kristal. He showered them with gifts, money and jewellery. Kristal owned three sports cars by the time she obtained her driver's licence. Malcolm's staff feared him a great deal. He had hired cutthroat mercenaries from other successful companies by compensating them royally in cash and stock. He handpicked his executives for their shrewdness, toughness, and ruthless, iron-fisted style. He set the pace and they followed. When he took over a competitor, he did not hesitate for a moment to lay off large numbers of people and break up their divisions as part of his policy of "fused integration." Malcolm always said, "You grow bigger by becoming smaller." He was also very ruthless in the manner in which he fired the staff, as he implemented his fused integration policy.

People who worked for Malcolm did so because they had to, not because they wanted to. As a rule, he made it a point to regularly threaten his employees and make them feel insecure, because he believed that fearful people produced the maximum.

He believed that employee insecurity was the best form of security in his company. No employee was allowed to get comfortable at Asher. The secretaries had the hardest time. They had to work long hours, juggle their children like balls in the air, and be at the beck and call of Malcolm's executives. The pay was good but, to benefit from that, they had no option but to accept the harsh rules of the company. Malcolm's style was characterised by the word "oppression." Everyone who worked for him had to know the meaning of the word "submission."

After the merger of Tennessee Electro-Chip into Asher, Joe experienced a major shock. Within weeks of completion of the acquisition, more than 400 out of his 600 employees were fired and handed their dismal severance packages. Malcolm had sent his mercenaries to do the hatchet job. Everything Malcolm did was directly opposite to Joe's principles and beliefs. Joe was deeply upset to see his organisation dismantled with such brute force. One of Malcolm's key hatchet men was a 50-year-old executive by the name of Sloan. The first thing that Sloan did when he went to his target assignment was to put a team of hungry lawyers on the scene to dig through all the corporate files. They dug up whatever "dirt" they could find on the employees. If there was no dirt, then they fabricated allegations. They then threatened and coerced people in Mafia-style interviews to speak against their colleagues. They did not hesitate to file lawsuits against employees who they thought would be difficult to crack. In this way, they laid off many employees inexpensively. Malcolm recovered part of his company acquisition costs by collecting moneys from the employees, the defendants of Malcolm's lawsuits. Many employees did not have sufficient money to defend themselves, and therefore had to accept default judgements, thereby losing their homes and property to the mighty Asher. The wolf pack of lawyers, who earned a percentage of the kill, freely fabricated their allegations knowing full well that their cases would never get to trial, since the poor defendants would be broke long before the process reached that far.

Sadly, Joe had the misfortune of witnessing the gross abuse of his staff at the hands of Sloan and his gang. Initially, he chose to remain silent and to keep to the terms of his agreement with Malcolm. At the time of entering into the transaction, Joe had no idea that he was going to be in bed with the American corporate and legal Mafia. As the fused integration progressed, Joe could no longer sit quietly and watch the abuse, extortion and inhumane treatment of his staff. He resolved to fight back. It was like David taking on Goliath. Of course, Sloan had done his homework on Joe and in no time, Joe was served with six-inch thick lawsuits in five different States, thus exposing him to an enormous cost of defending himself. Malcolm's style was to cut the veins of his victims in many places simultaneously, so as to cause them to bleed dry very quickly. The American legal system allowed him to deploy such tactics with no restriction. It was not a matter of right or wrong, innocent or guilty. It was a matter of who had the staying power in dollars. This was Malcolm's playground, where he and his mighty dollar thrived!

Joe was sued for millions of dollars. He was falsely accused of the most horrible acts, including being involved in fraudulent activities that were beyond anything he could have imagined. The predator lawyers had done a perfect fabrication job with respect to Joe's alleged crimes. To make matters worse, Sloan, in his classic mercenary style, sponsored terrible stories about Joe in the media, to make certain that Joe was fully discredited and pressured from every corner. At one time, Joe was a highly respected member of the Memphis business community. Now, everyone looked at him with suspicion. The power of the print had managed to erase Joe's credibility, even amongst his closest friends. Joe's uncle, who was in the news business, had always told him, "The media can build a positive reputation overnight, but it can also destroy an entire legacy in minutes." This had all come true for Joe, in the form of a living nightmare. Through this very difficult period, his wife Mary and sons Michael and Sam stuck by him, day in and day out. They were an incredible source of strength for Joe. They were his only true assets. Through the multiple lawsuits across the country, Joe could see that he would lose his entire net worth in defending himself. Although most of the accusations against him were pure fabrications, Joe knew that he did not have enough capital to see the whole battle through. But, he fought back with strength and conviction, to protect his reputation and dignity.

In the coming months, Joe's company was completely dismantled by Malcolm. By applying his Mafia-style tactics, Malcolm caused the weaker employees to squeal against their stronger colleagues, thus removing all the obstacles that lay in his path. Malcolm called such people "term deposits." Once they had delivered the goods, he dismissed them too. In the midst of the legal battle, Malcolm decided to meet Joe in order to persuade him to surrender and hand over all his assets to Asher. The two men met in Malcolm's boardroom, accompanied by their respective lawyers.

Joe said to Malcolm, "What you have done to me, my company and my employees is unforgivable. You stormed into our lives with false promises and destroyed everything that we had built. With all the wealth you have amassed in Asher, what difference could my company have possibly made to your net worth?"

Malcolm replied, "This is my business. I believe in Darwin's theory of 'Survival of the Fittest'. I have the power of the dollar and the more dollars I can amass, the more powerful I will be. We all have our own styles and tactics. I believe that every human being on this planet has a skeleton buried somewhere in his or her closet. So I use these skeletons to make them more agreeable. There is nothing wrong with that! What you consider to be a pathetic act is actually a business strategy. My fused integration programme works. I take over companies, shrink them to their core and fuse them into my starship company. I teach my people that we should become smaller as we grow bigger. Joe, have you ever seen a nuclear bomb? Do you know how much energy can be concentrated and packed into one single warhead? It is amazing! That's what I am building — an economic warhead."

Joe replied by asking, "Have you ever seen the faces of the men, women and children who get incinerated when one of these nuclear warheads explodes?"

Malcolm replied, "The thrill is in building and owning the warhead. That is power. If there are casualties on the way, so be it. After all, how many cattle go to the slaughterhouse each day? It's part of life. We all still enjoy our steaks, don't we? I see myself becoming one of the top ten richest men in the world. Give me five years. I am sure you and I will both be alive to see that day. You see, Joe, I have nothing against you. That's just business."

Joe, who was flabbergasted with Malcolm's insensitivity, replied, "How can you say that's just business? You destroyed the company I had worked night and day to build. You sued my employees and took away their homes because they could not afford the cost of defending themselves. You extorted people into perjuring themselves by giving false evidence against their colleagues. You deliberately sued me in so many States in order to bankrupt me. You blatantly lied about me in your lawsuit allegations, knowing full well that these cases would never go to trial and so you would not have to prove anything. You discredited me in the media and destroyed my reputation in the community. And, you say that's just business?"

Malcolm smiled and replied, "We all have our own styles. I leave nothing to chance. I destroy my prey completely. That's just the way it is in my jungle! Now, I did not invite you here to talk about my business methods. Someday, I will lecture about my strategies at business schools! But today, I am here to persuade you to surrender all your assets to me and I will set you free. I have done a search on your home and everything you own. In total, you are worth $2.2 million. Hand it all over to me and I will leave you alone. If you don't, I will destroy you and your family. That is for sure!"

Joe stood up from his seat and said, "In civilised societies, what you just said to me would be called extortion. I am not afraid of you or your mighty company. I will fight you to the bitter end!"

Malcolm calmly replied, "Joe, they all told me you were bull-headed. But, you are stupid as well. The taxman or the FBI has not investigated you yet. That is next on the menu. I know you say you are innocent, and you probably are. So how would you like to spend the next five years of your life trying to keep out of jail and fighting to prove your innocence?"

Joe walked out of the boardroom, disgusted. His last words to Malcolm were, "You can use your money. You can use the legal system. You can bring in the authorities. You can use all your power and might, but you will never break me! Everything I have done in my life has stood on solid foundations. In these foundations lie my pride, joy and spirit. Nothing that you can do can possibly break the core of my being."

Joe went home to join his family for the weekend. Malcolm boarded his private jet and flew to his family vacation home in the Caribbean, with his wife, Elena and daughter, Kristal. On the way back, the plane crashed along the coastline of Florida. Elena and Kristal died instantly. Malcolm was paralysed from head to foot and ended up living like a vegetable, on a life support system for twelve years. No one could do anything to help him. His mighty dollars were powerless. Fate had dealt him with his own card of fused integration. Through the paralysis, Malcolm physically shrank to half his original size! He certainly did not grow bigger as he became smaller! At his funeral, there were a mere six people. The once Great Malcolm Asher was buried in a cemetery in circumstances that gave true meaning to the word "pitiful."

After the plane crash, Sloan took over the management of Asher. He continued with his brutal, mercenary ways, until, one day, the authorities finally caught up with him. He was charged with extortion and blackmail and imprisoned for life. The legal system that he had so masterfully manipulated finally served him with his own medicine. His wolf pack of lawyers were also handed sentences of varying lengths. This brought an end to Asher Microchip Inc. through bankruptcy. In keeping with the laws of the Universe, what had gone around had indeed come around.

Joe rebuilt his business empire and grew to become a highly respected entrepreneur in the United States. He remembered all the lessons that he had learnt. In the years that followed, his business grew to a level where he had all the powers of the mighty dollar available to him. He used this might wisely to help the less fortunate all around the world. He fought hard to reform the American legal system in order to make it fair and equitable for the economically disadvantaged. He lectured at universities about wealth, power, oppression, ethics, compassion and socially responsible development. In one of his lectures, Joe remembered Malcolm. He said to his students, "If you take the primary colours and bring them together, you produce the colour white. I once had the misfortune of meeting a man who showed me the true colour of darkness! The colour black, which is synonymous with darkness, has the power to absorb white. Yet white has the power to change the colour of black completely, and make it white, forever! These are forces and *motivations* that life presents to us. The wise among us learn from them."

The story of Malcolm and Joe teaches us a great deal about the *motivations* of the two leaders. Some of the negative motivations and their consequent actions in this story include:

Malcolm's desire to emulate his father;
His greed and obsession with money;
His oppression and use of fear and insecurity to coerce his employees to perform;

His ruthless approach towards dismantling companies and
firing employees;
His oppressive and abusive legal tactics;
The use of extortion to achieve his goals;
And more.

It would be beneficial to take the time and make a more
complete list of all the negative motivations that we can find in
this story. Then, we can perform a similar exercise in the context
of what is actually happening in our own personal lives. The
results may be quite revealing!

Some examples of the *positive motivations* and their
consequences in this story include:

Joe's compassion and generosity towards others;
His care and sensitivity towards his staff;
His keen interest in listening to everyone he met;
His careful and positive use of economic power;
His desire to share the lessons of his life with others;
His family relationship and support;
His confidence and absence of fear in the face of
Malcolm's threats;
And more.

It would be beneficial to take the time and make a more
complete list of all the positive motivations that we can find in
this story. Then, we can perform a similar exercise in the context
of what is happening in our own personal lives.

Human nature is such that we easily succumb to the
temptation to abuse power when we have it. We become

oppressors very quickly, often without realising it. Malcolm's style of oppression was very deliberate and obvious. But, in our own homes, we often exercise oppression in the way we treat our spouses, children, friends, and loved ones. We exercise oppression in the workplace and in many other aspects of our lives.

Children can also demonstrate classic examples of oppression. If we take a look at a playground, we can often see severe oppression and cruelty being unleashed by children who are supposedly innocent. Playground cruelty can be very harsh and hurtful. In some instances, such oppression can leave permanent scars in the lives of these little beings. We should ask ourselves, "Where do the children, who oppress others, learn to do so?" One often needn't look further than one's very own home. To cite an example, when my daughter was ten years old, she was very different from the other children. She was more mature in her outlook towards everything. Therefore, she had no friends in her class. In the playground at her school, she tried to join the other children, but the leaders of their groups rejected and ignored her. The rest of the children in those groups dutifully followed. One day, I visited her school at lunchtime and found her sitting at a table all by herself, looking very sad. Her peers sat together at the next table, laughing and making fun of others. There was plenty of room at their table, but they deliberately excluded my daughter. This scene of harshness brought tears to my eyes.

"But, that is life," I said to myself. My daughter was a victim of oppression and exclusion by her peers. This experience has, unfortunately, left a mark in her that will take a long time to heal. When we look at children, we immediately think of their innocence. Yet, this is the very reason why oppression can be easily embedded into their little minds. If children, who are supposed to be innocent, can exercise oppression, then what chance do we as adults stand?

The lessons in this chapter reveal the fact that *oppression* can take many different forms and it creeps into our lives, often without our knowledge. *Oppression* is a significant source of conflict. When we find ourselves imposing our will upon others, we should stop and ask ourselves, "Am I acting like Malcolm?" When we find ourselves being pressured by others, we should pause and think about whether we are wilfully allowing ourselves to be oppressed. If not, what steps can we take to stop this oppression that we are suffering. Perhaps we should speak to our oppressor about it and if we do not succeed in reasoning with our oppressor, then, perhaps, we should step away from the relationship for a period of time. There are many ways to deal with oppression as long as we can recognise its existence.

For many, the natural inner response to *oppression* is fear, anger and hatred, which in themselves are destructive forces. *Oppression*, as exercised by the oppressor, is often born from anger, hatred and insecurity. Therefore, it is a self-fuelling conflict, which must be recognised and overcome. We should take stock of our own behaviour and attitudes to see if we are indeed acting as oppressors. If so, we should try to change our ways. We should say to ourselves, "He or she is my equal." Or, "I am not above anyone." With this recognition, we will be able to change our ways. Remember, if we stop being the oppressors, the conflict from *oppression*, which can spread like a forest fire, will come to an end. There will be no ignition available to light those destructive flames. If we can reach out to our families, friends and loved ones with an approach of zero-oppression, we will be able to teach them important lessons through our own example. This will take us one step closer *towards zero conflict*.

Seeds of Resolution

❀ Let us reflect upon the following thoughts:

"WE ARE ALL EQUAL.
NO ONE IS GREATER THAN THE OTHER.
EACH BEING IS BLESSED WITH A WILL THAT
IS WORTHY OF OUR RESPECT.
WE SHOULD NOT IMPOSE OUR WILL UPON
OTHERS.
NEITHER SHOULD WE ALLOW OTHERS TO
IMPOSE THEIR WILL UPON US.
WE SHOULD SHARE OUR COLLECTIVE WILL
IN HARMONY."

❀ Let us also contemplate and internalise the following seeds:

"I AM A FREE BIRD
SOARING THE SKIES.
I HOLD BACK NO ONE
AND LET NO ONE HOLD ME BACK
FOR FREEDOM IS THE GREATEST GIFT OF
ALL."

My Reflections

Now   date: /   /   .

My Reflections

One Year Hence   date: /   /   .

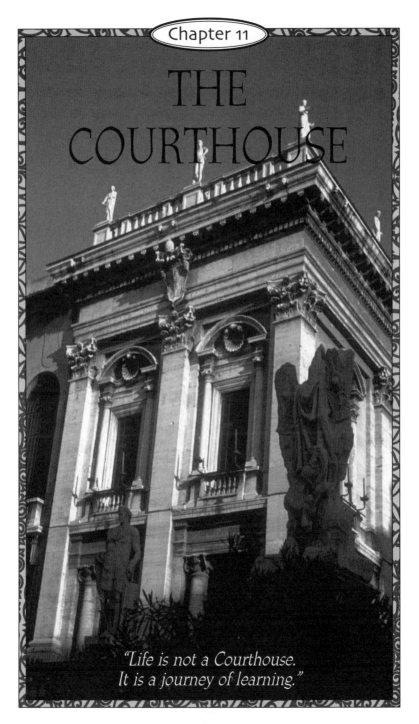

THE COURTHOUSE

*"Life is not a Courthouse.
It is a journey of learning."*

Judgements, opinions, biases and criticisms are a significant source of conflict that reside within us and can severely impact on all those around us. Each one of us has a mind full of opinions. We perceive people, things and events, and form instant opinions, which, in turn, influence our attitudes. We are also very quick to pass judgements on others based upon the few facts that we have about them or the perceptions that we have created. Our behaviour is largely governed by our judgements, biases and opinions. Some of us are very quick to make criticisms based on these opinions. These are all significant sources of inner and outer conflict that we need to understand and overcome. They are indeed sources of unhappiness, frustration, pain, anger and destruction, especially if our opinions and biases are predominantly of a negative nature. It is essential for us to realise that we can never ever know all there is to know about any person or thing.

A human being is like a piece of paper that is blank on one side and has the truth about him or her written on the other side. When we look at a person, all we see is the blank side of the paper. We may sometimes, if we are lucky, catch a glimpse of the truth that is written on the other side. Hence, we can never really know a person fully. Yet, based on minimal information, we form opinions or pass judgements on people from a position of pure ignorance. Therefore, nine times out of ten, we are wrong.

Our opinions and judgements shape our attitudes towards people. They shape how we feel about them and how we treat them. Is it not a frightening thought that our attitudes and behaviour are driven by opinions that are incorrect more than 90 percent of the time? In Chapter 5, the story of the two Martians, Ozzie and Commie, clearly illustrated the difference that exists between perception and reality.

Some of us can also be very harsh in the way we make use of our opinions. We quickly judge people, formulate our opinions about them, and then go around spreading our views by convincing others that we are correct. In this way, we spread our ignorance in many directions, and in doing so, we impact the lives of people in such a dramatic way, creating unimaginable conflicts as a result. The tragic part is that very few of us ever realise how wrong we are about our opinions and judgements. We must ask the question, "How can we learn to stop judging others?" The following story provides insights that will help us to better understand the conflicts that we create as a result of our opinions, judgements and biases.

THE MINER'S SON

One bright, sunny morning in the year 1969, Jannie, the 13-year-old son of a middle-class white family in Pretoria headed towards his school. These were the times of apartheid in South Africa, where government policies prohibited the free integration of black, white and coloured people. Each group was required to stay within their own confines and social circles. They were not allowed to share ideas, things, places or events. Jannie had been brought up to believe that white people were a class of their own, who had to stick together and maintain their boundaries from black and coloured people. To

Jannie, this was a way of life, the only way of life he had known. He was raised to believe that black and coloured people were subservient to white people, which gave him a sense of authority over them, by virtue of the rules of the society he grew up in.

The route to Jannie's school took him through a little bush trail that bypassed the main commercial areas of Pretoria. That morning, as he happily strolled towards the school, he heard a rustling noise in the bushes. Before he knew it, he was standing in front of a tall, dark wildebeest that was pounding its feet angrily into the ground. It had been wounded, and in this state, it was very dangerous. A stream of blood flowed down the side of its neck. Someone had shot the poor animal in the head. The beast stared at Jannie and then charged at him. Jannie was terrified and froze. He felt a surge of pain in his thigh as the wildebeest knocked him down. He lay helplessly on the ground. The beast turned around, ready to charge at him once more. Just then, Jannie noticed a youth scream and run straight towards the beast. The boy hurled a rock that hit the animal precisely over the bullet wound on its head. The animal turned around in agony and darted off into the bush. A few moments later, there was a loud thud as the wildebeest collapsed on the ground. The beast had succumbed to the fatal bullet wound.

The youth who saved Jannie was around 15 years old. He was the son of a black miner who worked in the gold mines of Johannesburg. His name was Stan. He was out running an errand for his mother and had taken the bush trail. Luckily, he saw the wounded wildebeest attack Jannie. He dropped his grocery bag on the ground, picked up a rock and charged towards the animal, with no fear for his own safety. All he was concerned about was saving Jannie. Stan walked over to Jannie, who was moaning with pain and asked, "Are you all right?"

"Yes, thanks," replied Jannie. Stan noticed that Jannie's thigh was bleeding profusely. Without a moment's hesitation, he ripped apart his shirtsleeve and made a bandage, which he tied around Jannie's leg. Jannie watched all this with a mixture of fear, pain and gratitude. Stan helped Jannie up and accompanied him back towards his home. Jannie looked at the courageous dark boy and said, "Thank you for saving my life. Are you aware that the wildebeest could have killed you?"

Stan replied, "Yes, but I had to save you."

Amazed at this remark, Jannie then said, "But I am white and you do not even know me! By the way, my name is Jannie."

Jannie held his hand out in greeting to his saviour who replied, "My name is Stan. My father is a miner at the gold mines. He goes three kilometres below each day to dig up the gold rocks. He always says to me, 'Son, when you go down into that mine, it is very, very dark. It is so dark that you cannot see your own hand when the lights are off. At three kilometres below the ground, you cannot tell who is black or who is white. We are all people, working together. When the earth shakes or the walls of the mine start to cave in, we rush to rescue one another. We are there for each other.' So, Jannie, I learned from my father that I must be there for others, whether it be three kilometres under the ground or in the bush out here."

Jannie was silent for a moment and then said, "You are a wonderful person, Stan. I have always been told that black people are not to be trusted. I have been told not to be friends with them. They steal and they are unreliable. Believe it or not, every time I see a black person, that is what I think. Yet, here you are, Stan, having risked your own life to save a white stranger, whom you know nothing about! My opinions about your people were wrong and I apologise for that. Can we be friends?"

Stan smiled and replied, "Yes, indeed, we can be friends. Like you, I have heard about white people from my friends, who say that they are greedy and not to be trusted. They say white people are two-faced, cruel and ungrateful. They say we can never be friends with white people. Yet my father is different. He always talks about people, as just people. He says that all people are equal and deserve love, care and friendship."

The two boys finally reached Jannie's home. Stan knocked on the door and Jannie's mother, Eve, looked through the window before opening the door. She was horrified to see Jannie covered in blood. The first thought that came to her mind was that the black boy had attacked her son for she had grown up to judge black people as thieves and muggers. She opened the door and came rushing out, screaming and hurling insults at Stan. Within minutes, a crowd of white people had gathered around Jannie and Stan. One of them had grabbed Stan by the arms and pinned him against the wall. Jannie was shocked by the display of hostility towards the boy who had saved his life and shouted, "Stop! Don't hurt him!" The crowd went silent and listened shamefully as Jannie explained what had happened. He concluded by saying to all present that Stan was now a friend and a brother to him. He owed his life to Stan. Jannie's mother was the first to go over to Stan, who was shaking like a leaf with fright, put her arms around him, and thanked him for saving her son's life. The neighbours apologised to Stan and then left.

Eve took Jannie and Stan into her home. She nursed her son's wounds with Stan's help. As she looked at the courageous, yet innocent little black boy, she said to herself, "How wrong can we all be about one another!"

———————

Here is a classic example of how people judge others and display their opinions, biases and prejudices. In this story, there was an element of racial, cultural and social bias that influenced the white people. They immediately judged Stan as a criminal and an aggressor, simply because he was black. Stan could have left Jannie to die had he listened to his friends' opinions, biases and prejudices against the white people. It was the wisdom of his father, gained while mining three kilometres into the belly of the earth, that saved Jannie's life!

THE MOMBASA CAFÉ

In the summer of 1988, my best friend, Robert, from Canada, and I visited Kenya for a safari tour. He was very excited about being in the wilderness of Africa to experience a world that was very different to his. Before starting our safari, we decided to spend a few days in Mombasa, along the coast of the Indian Ocean. Mombasa is a city with a rich cultural history, since it has been colonised and inhabited by many different peoples including the migratory African Bantu tribe, the Omani Arabs, the Portuguese and the British. Robert looked forward to savouring the historical experience of Mombasa, as well as basking in the sunshine on its pure, white, sandy beaches. Two days after our arrival in Kenya, we sat in the patio of the Mombasa Café, having a leisurely late morning breakfast and watching the world go by. The streets were fairly crowded with pedestrians, merchants and hawkers. Suddenly, I heard Robert swear and point at two local Swahili boys who walked past us holding hands. "These damned gays are everywhere!" Robert exclaimed, with a look of total disgust on his face. "They should be shot! I thought they only existed in Canada!"

I looked at Robert, surprised at his hostile reaction towards the two boys, who, after all, were minding their own business. I asked Robert, "What do you have against gay people?"

He replied, "I don't know, I just find them disgusting. They make me sick! I mean, with all the beautiful women in the world, why would men want to do it with one another? The entire notion makes me sick."

I was intrigued with Robert's comments and felt like taking the conversation a step further. I said, "Robert, did you know that in the days of Aristotle, homosexuality amongst men was the norm in Greece? I mean, Aristotle has been quoted in his writings as saying that he was honoured when his teacher offered to make love to him. So, in his society, homosexuality was a perfectly normal and accepted practice."

Robert looked at me as if I had lost my mind. "Right now, we are in Mombasa and the year is 1988. I don't give a damn about Aristotle and the Greeks. I have paid a lot of money to come and enjoy my holiday in Kenya. I came to see the wildlife and the scenery, not to look at a bunch of gays walking down Mombasa's streets!"

By this time, I thought I should let Robert in on a secret. I said, "Robert, you know that I grew up here, don't you?"

He looked up at me with a strange expression and said, "Don't tell me you too are gay!"

I laughed and replied, "Don't worry, Robert, I am not gay and if I were gay, I would have picked a better-looking guy than you!"

Robert laughed and then said, "You were going to tell me something, weren't you?"

I replied, "Yes, Robert. You see, in Kenyan culture, it is perfectly normal for friends to hold hands with one another. Boys hold hands with boys and girls hold hands with girls. This is how friendship is expressed here. It doesn't make them gay or lesbian. I mean, I used to hold hands with my friends until I turned 16. Then I went to the U.K. to study where I learnt that it was taboo to do so."

Robert looked a little embarrassed by his instant judgement of the two boys. He then said, "Well, I'm sorry I jumped to conclusions so quickly."

I then asked, "Robert, when you were at kindergarten, did you not hold hands with your friends, regardless of whether they were boys or girls?"

He replied, "Yes, I guess so."

I then asked, "So, what's changed?"

Robert replied, "I guess as I grew up. I learned about gays and lesbians and began to dislike them."

I asked him another question, "Who told you they were bad people? How did you develop this dislike for them?"

He replied, "My dad hated homosexuals. During the war, when he was in the navy, he used to go around with his friends beating up gay sailors. Also, amongst my group of friends, we always talked about homosexuals as people who were not acceptable in our society. So I developed a bias towards them and this bias grew into hatred. I can't help the way I feel about it."

I then said, "Robert, I am not gay, but let us suppose for a moment that after knowing me for all these years as your best friend, you found out that I was gay. Would you forget all the good things about me and our friendship, and start hating me?"

Robert paused and said, "I don't know. I mean, I have always respected you and learnt so much from you. So I would not say that being gay makes you a bad person. But seriously, I don't know how I would react!"

I thought I should test Robert's feelings further on this issue. So, I asked him, "Robert, you are so fond of your mother and you love her very much. What if you found out one day that she had lesbian tendencies?"

Robert frowned, shook his head and replied, "Man oh man! I would freak out! That's for sure!"

I then said, "But think about it for a moment. Your mum is such a wonderful woman. Would you forget all the special things about her and start hating her because of her sexual preference?"

Robert had no answer. He stood up and said, "I've come here for a fun safari, not to think about my best friend being a homosexual or my mother being a lesbian! Let's go and check out the rest of Mombasa."

In that brief conversation between two friends, we can see how our strong biases can surface, sometimes in a manner that can be unpleasant. Isn't it interesting to see how quickly Robert branded the two boys, who were holding hands, as being gay? Isn't it interesting to see how he harboured such strong emotions and feelings within himself against homosexuality as a result of his father's attitude and bias? These feelings were unhealthy for Robert since they were a source of conflict for him. The questions that I asked him were penetrating in nature and he did not know how to handle his feelings once his prejudice against homosexuals, based on shallow foundations, was exposed.

From my perspective, making him aware of his prejudice and getting him to think about it was a very healthy exercise. He also realised how quick he was to pass judgement on others. He knew nothing about the local culture and how the simple act of holding hands was an expression of friendship and not sexual preference. Robert had obviously been conditioned to think differently, within the context of his North American upbringing.

He enjoyed his Kenyan safari and returned to Canada with the question about his prejudice against homosexuals still lingering at the back of his mind.

Five years later, when we met in Vancouver, he brought up the subject again. It was interesting for me to learn that during the five-year period, he had frequently prodded his feelings on this issue and reflected about his prejudice. Through this process, he had learnt to become more accepting towards peoples' sexual preferences. I smiled as I thought about how a 30-minute chat in an outdoor cafe in Mombasa, had changed the outlook of my dear friend Robert, on the issue of homosexuality.

We are all surrounded by live stimuli on so many issues like poverty, racial prejudice, homosexuality, AIDS, abortion, crime, violence against women, drugs, exploitation, etc. etc. We all develop and hold our own biases on these matters. For example, I remember a group discussion in a restaurant in Reno, where my friend Warren jokingly asked his buddy, Tim, "When did you stop beating your wife?"

Tim frowned and replied, "I'm not even married! I don't have a wife!"

We all laughed at this exchange. Yet each time I saw Tim after that, I thought about him beating his girlfriend. I wonder how many of my friends in the group looked at Tim in this way after that day. It is interesting how simple conversations leave impressions within us that later grow into in-built opinions. From that day, the word spread and Tim soon found his place in Reno's top-ten list of wife beaters! Nothing he could say or do could change this "fact" now.

We judge people all the time based on their race, colour, height, weight, personality, lifestyle, social status, etc. But, do we really know the people whom we are judging? Remember the piece of paper that is blank on one side and written on the other? The side that bears the truth about a person is never visible to the eye. How then can we truly know someone to be able to judge him or her? We may think we know someone well, but we are wrong more often than we are right. Also, we should remember that the written side of the page, which we cannot see, is written upon every day. The knowledge within the person grows every day. People change each and every day. Therefore, judging people is, indeed a fatal mistake! What gives one person the authority to judge another person?

Why can we not live our lives in peace and happiness without taking on the stress and pressure of judging others? Would it not be wonderful to just be? Would it not be fascinating to accept people as they are and discover the rich mysteries that reside within them? Would it not be special to view people as bearers of gifts of knowledge, wisdom and experience? Every moment, we are presented with the wonderful opportunity to learn from those whom we encounter. Judgements and opinions build walls around us and the precious knowledge that we can gain from others is shut away from us permanently.

Therefore, we should strive to take a neutral position about people, things and events. We should keep an open mind and try to learn from all the little and large experiences of life. With this neutral attitude we will be able to eliminate a great deal of stress, pressure and conflict from within. In turn, our neutral attitude will help eliminate conflicts that would normally be created with others through our judgements, opinions, biases and prejudices. We can become like magnets that attract the knowledge and beauties from everything around us. Would that not be a highly enriching experience? Learning to recognise when we are being judgemental, and letting go of our prejudices will help us to take huge strides towards a state of *zero conflict*. Let us always remind ourselves, *"Life is not a courthouse. It is a journey of learning."*

Seeds of Resolution

❁ Let us contemplate and internalise the following seeds:

"I SHALL NOT JUDGE.

FOR, I KNOW NOTHING ABOUT THOSE
WHOM I JUDGE.

I HONOUR THE BLANK SIDE
OF THEIR PAGE OF LIFE.

AND PRAY TO DISCOVER THE WRITINGS
ON THE OTHER SIDE.

BY GRATEFULLY ACCEPTING THE GIFTS
OF LEARNING THEY BRING."

On April 7, 2002, I was blessed with a beautiful inspiration in a rose garden in Malaga, which I am honoured to share in this book.

An Inspired Message from a Rose About Judgement

I look into the sky, as the warm rays of the morning sun
Bless the earth and bring everything to life.
On the ground, there are dewdrops
That carry within them the secrets of the night.

I am in a rose garden
Filled with roses of all types, colours and fragrances.
I look at a young, red rosebud that is just beginning to unfold.
I marvel at its deep, red colour
And imagine the beautiful red rose that is to emerge.
I can only but imagine the fragrance that it is to carry.

I announce to those whom I encounter
The arrival of this precious red rose.
I announce to the world the arrays of shades of red
That it is to embody.
I announce to the world the depth of the fragrance it is to carry.

The day has now come to an end and I embrace the night
With the rest that it brings to my tired eyes.

Once again at sunrise
I walk into the garden to greet the red rose
That I had so dearly awaited.

But, to my surprise, I find no red rose.
The bud has indeed blossomed
But the rose is not red.

It is yellow.
With infinite shades of colour
Flowing into one another.
The tips of its petals are pink
Which is all that remains of the red that I had imagined.

How could I have been so wrong?
After all, what I had seen was indeed a red rosebud.
But within it lay the promise of a yellow rose
And not the one that I had so boldly
announced to the world.

Can I ever judge anything anymore?
Can I truly ever know the secrets
that lie behind all that I see?

I am born in a world full of rosebuds.
I am born in a world full of people.
I am born in a world full of creation.
How can I ever judge anything anymore?
How can I ever judge anyone anymore?
I can only but await each rosebud
To reveal its brilliant secret.
That may fill my heart with joy
For life is indeed a journey of joy...

My Reflections

Now   date: / /   .

My Reflections

One Year Hence   date: / / .

Chapter 12

JEALOUSY

Jealousy arises from inadequacy...

Jealousy is a powerful negative motivation *that can cause untold pain and damage. Jealousy arises from inadequacy. It starts as a feeling or emotion that grows exponentially, if permitted. Jealousy creates inner pain and anxiety, giving birth to forces of destruction within its victims. Uncontrolled jealousy has the power to grow into an obsession, causing even more pain. Envy is the sister-force of jealousy that is inherently embodied within jealousy. Whilst one cannot tell them apart, their combined impact can be very damaging.*

Jealousy brings destruction to all that comes in its way. People who are jealous burn with inner turmoil, causing damage to their health whilst losing precious moments of life in the midst of their unhealthy inner storms. The victims of jealous people suffer a great deal of harm, which adds to the flame of conflict. The net effect is cyclones of negative whirlwinds that tear apart everything that comes in their way.

Jealousy usually manifests in people who are insecure, unsure of themselves, despondent and overly concerned about how they are perceived by their fellow beings. People who harbour jealousy are not usually at peace with themselves and with their surroundings. They are not content with what they possess and spend a great deal of their energies trying to be who they are not. They constantly strive to obtain what others have, in order to fill the void that exists within them. Unfortunately, this is a void that cannot be satisfied by anything in this world.

There are many reasons why people suffer from jealousy. For some, it is a basic personality trait of a highly sensitive nature. For others, it is the result of depravation during childhood, being treated unfairly, being bullied, or emulating people who harbour jealousy. Whatever the cause, it is important that jealousy is eliminated from one's life, in order to bring about peace, cordial relations, harmony and success. The best way to eliminate jealousy is to firstly recognise its existence within and then to change one's outlook and attitudes, both internally and externally. Understanding the purpose of one's life on earth will take one a long way towards overcoming jealousy.

I recall a conversation with my friend, Glenn, who suffered from a deep-rooted jealousy towards his family and friends. This jealousy had cost him his marriage and had left him isolated from his friends and loved ones. He could not pinpoint the problem but realised that the problem lay within him, and that he needed to do something about it. Therefore, he came to me for advice.

After listening to his long and painful story about how things had fallen apart in his life, it became clear to me that the root cause of his problem was jealousy and envy.

Before I shared my opinion, I asked him a simple question, "Glenn, imagine that you were a short tree in a forest alongside taller trees, and you wanted to be taller than your neighbours, what would you do?"

Without giving my question any thought, Glenn immediately replied, "I would cut the other trees down so that they would become smaller than me."

I replied, "Instead of doing that, why not try to grow taller than the others, while allowing them to live freely also?"

He replied, "That would take too long and require a lot of work. Besides, how would I go about growing taller than the others?"

I replied, "Therein lies your problem, Glenn. You think it is easier to cut the others down so that you can get ahead. But, in doing so, you are playing with a sharp, double-edged blade that cuts both ways. Your victim bleeds while you feel the pain!"

I continued, "As to the question about growing taller than the others, the key lies in being able to see life from a different perspective. You are jealous of others because you believe that they are better than you and that they have more than you. Your envy towards them breeds suspicion too, and hence, you trust no one. You act in a manner that causes discomfort to others and therefore, they opt to keep away from you. For instance, your loved ones, who tried hard to help you, gave up because the harder they tried, the more you alienated yourself from them. I know that this could not have been easy for you. Glenn, to grow taller than the others, you have to tap into the infinite richness that exists within yourself. You are far greater from within than you realise. If you believe that you are everything, and everything is you, then there is no room for inadequacy. One who is everything is content and seeks nothing from others. Such a person discovers richness within and around himself or herself."

I continued, "But, my dear friend, these are not just words. You have to internalise them into every single cell in your body. You have to be filled with this understanding, because only when you are filled can you fulfil."

I believe that our conversation helped Glenn. He decided that he was going to follow my advice and meditate upon the words and thoughts that I had shared with him. Glenn needed to recognise that the root cause of his problems was his jealousy and envy, which was inherent in his personality trait, exacerbated by the circumstances of his upbringing. He always reacted in a destructive manner to events that arose because of this root cause. I believe that recognising such conflicts within us represents 50 percent of the solution to overcoming it.

People who are confident, believe in their capabilities, and understand that life is a journey to be experienced holistically, are less prone to harbour jealousy. They are self-assured and know that whatever they gain or lose in this life is part of the process of learning from life's experiences. They recognise that whatever they receive comes from their Origin, or Source, and that there is a perfect purpose behind each and every blessing they receive. Such people are at peace with themselves and their surroundings.

The following story reveals dimensions of jealousy and their impact, offering us valuable food for contemplation.

THE FALLEN STAR

*Our desires are a fertile breeding ground
for jealousy and envy.*

The curtains came down. The show was over. This was Melanie's last performance as a singer. Her agreement with the theatre had come to an end, which was not going to be renewed. The crowd left the auditorium quietly. Nobody waited to greet the great star or ask for an autograph.

Melanie walked alone to her car in the deserted car park. This day had brought a sense of finality to her. She felt sad and lonely. At one time, she was surrounded by thousands of fans that were happy to just catch a glimpse of her. Wherever she went, people crowded around her, begging for a handshake or an autograph. But now, it was all over. The spot lights had been turned off and for Melanie, the rest of her life seemed like one long, dark night that would never end.

She drove through the back streets of Salt Lake City to the highway that led to her beautiful log cabin in the mountains, where she usually spent her free time. She took the usual exit off the highway, which led to a dark, narrow winding trail towards the cabin. She was tired, depressed, and not in a condition to drive through the perilous mountain roads. A few moments later, her car suddenly sped around a sharp bend and skidded off the road. She heard a loud bang as the car slammed into the metal barrier at the edge of the road, alongside a steep cliff. The barrier gave way and the car plunged at least a thousand feet down the cliff. Melanie drifted in and out of consciousness. Her head throbbed with pain and the world around her seemed to be spinning out of control. Then, all of a sudden, everything stopped and the world turned silent.

She found herself gliding in the sky, like an eagle, in the still, dark night. She looked below and saw the wreckage of her car at the foot of the cliff. She did not know what was happening, but she felt calm and peaceful, despite her state of mind prior to the accident. She looked to her side and was awestruck with the sight of a group of golden eagles that had come to join her. The eagles had beautiful, human faces! Melanie was stunned and frightened. "Where am I?" She thought to herself. "What is happening here?"

Miraculously, she heard a soothing voice. It sounded very much like her mother who had died some ten years previously. The voice said, "Melanie, you are free now. You are light now and you carry no burdens anymore. When you are ready, you can fly with us to your home in the Golden Sky."

In front of her, Melanie saw a tender, gentle, face of a woman, who must have been around 50 years old. She had the body of an eagle and her golden wings flapped graciously in the still, dark night. Her face had a radiance Melanie had never seen before. Melanie asked in a quiet, nervous voice, "Who are you and where am I?"

The woman replied, "I am Sitara, your guide, who has been sent to show you the way home when you are ready. Look below you. There is the car in which you crashed and died. You are free now. Don't you love your wings? Don't you just adore the liberating feeling as you fly?"

Melanie felt a sense of comfort and happiness. She replied, "Yes, it feels wonderful. I feel happy, warm and loved. I have not felt this way for a long time."

Sitara then said, "Yes, Melanie. I know your life was like a roller coaster. You rose to the peak in your career and enjoyed the fame and glory that came with it. You flew across the world like a shooting star."

Sitara continued, "Then came your downfall, for it was time for you to land. It was time for you to come back to reality, and what a harsh reality that was! You felt hurt, pain and rejection, all of which you created as a result of the way you lived. You were the architect of your own pains. Now that you are free, it feels good. I will lead you to the Golden Sky when you are ready."

Melanie asked, "My dear Sitara, what is the Golden Sky and when am I supposed to be ready?"

Sitara replied, "The Golden Sky is a place of peace, happiness and Light. It is a place that is infinite, for you cannot see where it begins or where it ends. In the Golden Sky resides a depth of love and warmth that you could never experience in your lifetime on earth. In the Golden Sky, we have no form. We are just Beings. We are Light."

Melanie inquired, "When can we go there? It must be a truly beautiful place."

Sitara replied, "You must learn the lessons that you failed to learn during your lifetime. When you have done so, I will lead you there."

Melanie looked at the other golden eagles that flew beside Sitara and asked, "Who are they?"

Sitara replied, "They are guides like me who are on their way to receive those whom they are to guide. As I told you, in the Golden Sky, we have no form. But, when we travel, we take whatever form we choose. Today we are eagles."

Melanie then asked, "What must I learn before I can go to the Golden Sky?"

With a concerned expression on her face, Sitara replied, "Look back at your life since you were a child. You were never happy. You always looked at others and wanted the things they had. You were a very jealous child. I want you to think about the jealousy. Why did you feel that way?"

Melanie had never given thought to this very difficult question before. She replied, "I felt inadequate all the time. I always thought I had nothing of my own. I wanted everything I saw, because I felt that having everything would make me feel complete. But, I could never get everything I wanted, and it left a painful void in me. When I saw what the others had, I felt upset because they had what I did not. I hated them for it, and yearned to grab for myself, everything that they had. When I could not do that, it made me angry and frustrated. I felt that if I could not have what they had, then they shouldn't have it either! So, in my anger and hatred for them, which was fuelled by my jealousy, I did everything I could to tear them down! As a result, nobody wanted to be my friend, because they thought I was strange. Nobody even wanted to come close to me, and this made me feel lonely and bitter."

With a warm, understanding smile, Sitara replied, "Yes it was the jealousy and envy which caused you to hurt intensely, and to hurt all those around you even more. It made you repulsive, and thus, nobody wanted to be close to you. But, from the Golden Sky, you were given an opportunity to have everything that you wished for, later in your life. You were blessed with the wealth that you yearned for; the handsome man of your dreams you coveted; the fame that came with your stardom; the satisfaction of feeling wanted by everyone; and so much more! Why did all that not change you? After receiving all that you wanted, why were you still not happy? Why, did you then do the horrible things that followed?"

Melanie replied, "My jealousy was like a fire that could not be extinguished. It was like a thirst that could not be quenched. As I received the things that I wished for, the void in me still remained. Then, I did not want anybody but myself to have it all. That was my envy. I was a star, a success story; a somebody. But, each time I looked at Sylvia, who sang so beautifully, and won the hearts of so many, it made me angry! I asked myself, "Why should she have such a gift?" It made me hate her, and I wanted to take the gift away from her. Each time I looked at her, the fire inside of me blazed with a heat that scorched my soul."

Sitara then said, "So you poisoned Sylvia. You spiked her drink with a potion that destroyed her voice."

Ashamed, Melanie replied, "Yes. That is true."

Sitara then asked, "Melanie, you had everything you could ever dream of. You won all the hearts you ever wanted to. So, why then did you do such a harsh thing?"

Melanie replied," It was my jealousy, my envy. I carried it in me from childhood and even after gaining fame and success, it did not leave me. I know now that only I could have extinguished the flames of jealousy within me."

Sitara then said, "All you had to do was to say to yourself each day, *I have much to be grateful for. I have everything. I*

am everything.' These words would have helped to put out
the flames of jealousy and envy, for if you had indeed
believed that you were *everything*, then the success of others
would have brought you joy, not misery. The success of others
would have been your success. *If you are everything, then
everything is you."*

With deep regret in her voice, Melanie replied, "I wish I had
heard your words of wisdom sooner. My life could have been so
different. I would not have fallen from grace the way that I did.
All along, I had the power in me to overcome jealousy and envy.
But I did not use it. If only I had heard your words, *'You are
everything and everything is you'* and understood them fully,
cherished and internalised them, I would have been a very
different person."

Sitara then said, "Remember, I told you that we will go to the
Golden Sky when you were ready. You have learnt your lesson.
Now, you may go back into your wrecked car and live for
another five years. In that time, you will correct all the wrongs
that you have done. You will travel around the world and share
with everyone what you have learnt. You will teach people how
to extinguish the flames of jealousy and envy. You will teach
them to say each day *'I am everything and everything is me.'* By
living your life in this manner, completely free of jealousy and
envy, you will find great joy and happiness over the next five
years. This is not a joy that comes from fame and fortune. It is a
happiness that comes from the enrichment of your soul. This
happiness carries the diamonds, rubies, and pearls that blossom
in your every thought, which you will share freely with the
world. Once you have learnt to share freely and experience the
joy in doing so, you will be ready to fly to the Golden Sky. I will

be waiting for you Melanie, with my wings wide open to embrace you as the next golden eagle."

The story of Melanie and Sitara gives us a special insight into jealousy. It describes the consequences of jealousy and envy. It helps us to understand and recognise our own jealousies. It teaches us to understand this powerful *negative motivation* and to assist those who may be jealous of us. Overcoming jealousy and envy, which are major sources of conflict, takes us one step closer *towards zero conflict.*

Seeds of Resolution

❀ Let us contemplate and internalise the following seeds:

"I AM FREE OF JEALOUSY

FOR I AM EVERYTHING

AND EVERYTHING IS ME.

I LACK NOTHING

FOR I AM ABUNDANCE

AND ABUNDANCE IS ME..."

My Reflections

Now   date: /   /   .

My Reflections

One Year Hence   date: /   /   .

My Reflections

Chapter 13

SEXUALITY

"Sexuality is a power of self-expression."

Sexuality is a blessing that is bestowed upon all living things. It is a natural mechanism for procreation. Among human beings, however, sexuality needs to be viewed from a perspective that goes beyond basic procreation. When we were children, we looked upon our own sexuality with curiosity, fascination, concern and sometimes obliviousness, depending upon our background, culture and religious beliefs. Some of us found the concept of sexuality and sexual intercourse somewhat disgusting and intimidating.

Of course, as we grew up and matured physically, the hormones took over! We began to experience a physical attraction towards others and in the earlier stages, this attraction sometimes took the form of a powerful infatuation. There were beautiful feelings of joy when our infatuation was fulfilled, and pain, when our attraction was not reciprocated. Many of us spent a great deal of time thinking about these feelings. We dreamt and imagined the fulfilment of our infatuations. We often lived in worlds of our own that were far removed from reality. This was all a process through which our sexuality developed. While our organs evolved in preparation for procreation, our feelings and emotions took on a deeper and often broader dimension. This was all part of the "experience" that life brings.

Then, as we learnt more, infatuation was replaced by the pure and wonderful feelings of love. This love took on a reality of its own. It manifested as powerful feelings and emotions that overtook the cool, calm, logical, decisions of our mind. We began to think with our hearts. The decisions of the heart are driven by love, not logic. This love, from the perspective of sexuality, needed to have a form of expression, which predominantly resulted in the act of lovemaking. The entire process was one of pleasure and fulfilment, if we were fortunate enough to have received reciprocal love from our beloved one. Sometimes, we were not so fortunate and our love was not accepted or reciprocated. This resulted in pain and hurt, which remained for a long time, perhaps even for a lifetime.

Let us examine the motivations that influence our sexual behaviour. Within the context of sexuality, 'desire' is a feeling or emotion that takes the form of a powerful need within us, constantly crying out for fulfilment. Desire is a powerful motivation, which can be both positive and negative. It can be a source of conflict within us. Desire is a part of the process of expressing our love. It becomes a positive motivation when our love is reciprocated, bringing joy and happiness. However, if our love is not reciprocated, the desire can manifest in the form of anger, hurt, jealousy, hatred and other negative motivations. It can become a destructive force, which can result in a great deal of inner pain to us and to others.

Desire, when associated with love and affection, represents a form of motivation that is usually positive in nature. This is called love desire. Whilst the overall process of love desire may involve sex, it is not the sole driving force. Numerous aspects of love are engaged in this process. Of course, there are instances where love desire can take on negative undertones. However, more often than not, love desire is positive and healthy.

The other form of desire *is a pure, raw, sexual motivation that is driven by animal instincts. This is called* lust desire. *It can be a very powerful force that often takes the form of a* negative motivation. *This raw sexual* desire *resides in the mind and sometimes becomes a sickness.*

Lust desire *tends to dominate people who do not release the built-up energies within them, through sports or physical activity. It can also influence people whose minds are bored, idle and unchallenged, particularly in the case of younger men and women. Of course, television, promiscuity and pornography, serve to fuel this desire further. If* lust desire *is not controlled, it can manifest in the form of physical violence, abuse, rape, emotional abuse and other such negative phenomena.*

As parents, we need to be on the lookout for the development of lust desire *in our children. We need to be open and allow our children to talk about their sexual feelings. The mere ability to talk about these feelings is therapeutic in itself. We should also be vigilant about what our children are doing with the wonderful reservoir of energy that is building up within them each day. Do they have an outlet for these energies? Do they play sports? Do they exercise enough? Releasing the built-up energies within them goes a long way towards preventing or overcoming the negative aspects associated with* lust desires. *If they are very busy and have little time to be bored or to think about these matters, then there is a good chance that they will be shielded from this negative desire. In addition, if children were imparted with a better understanding of their sexuality, they may, as a result, exercise it in a manner that is healthy, positive and responsible.*

It is important for us all to analyse and recognise our own feelings with respect to our lust desires and love desires. How dominant a role do these desires play in our lives? Are they positive or negative motivations for us? Do they cause us to hurt others or ourselves? Do they make us feel happy or miserable? Do we have fulfilment or do we lack fulfilment? If we lack fulfilment, what are we doing about it? How is this affecting us and those around us? We need to take time to reflect on these very important matters.

STRENGTHENING LOVE THROUGH MEDITATION

Let us consider practical ways of dealing with our *love desires* and *lust desires*, starting with *love desires*. If we are in a relationship where we give love and receive love in return, then we are fulfilled and happy. If we are in a relationship that is not balanced, for example, we are giving more than we are receiving, then we experience only partial fulfilment. In this case, what can we do to gain complete fulfilment? One option is to talk to our partner and express our feelings openly on the matter. This is not always easy since such openness does not exist in all relationships.

Sometimes, the problem may be that we are clinging too tightly to our loved one. We may be receiving love in return but we may feel that it is not enough. We need to ask ourselves if we are clinging too tightly or expecting too much.

If we are feeling unfulfilled in our *love desire*, it would be beneficial to take some time each day to sit quietly and contemplate on the matter. The following three meditations will assist in this process.

Meditation of Reaffirmation

You can start the meditation by sitting quietly and comfortably, and breathing freely. Take a few moments to relax your mind and body. When you feel ready, repeat the following words quietly to yourself, *"I love my partner."* You may insert the name of your partner in this statement.

Repeat this statement for two to three minutes. You may take longer if you wish. Think of the feelings of happiness that you share with your partner while repeating the words, *"I love my partner."* Keep your unhappy feelings towards your partner out of this process. Only focus on your happy feelings and re-affirm your love towards him or her as you recite these words. Smile to yourself as you repeat these words. After the two- to three-minute Reaffirmation Meditation, pause and sit quietly in preparation for the next meditation.

Meditation of Freedom

Continue to sit in a relaxed position and now, close your eyes and breathe freely. Imagine that you are looking at a golden birdcage that is in front of you. It is a beautiful cage with gentle, rounded edges. In this cage is a magnificent white dove, which is looking through the wires of the cage at you, with warm, loving eyes. Take a few moments and look at this bird, for it is indeed a representation of your loved one.

The dove looks happy to be in its cage, as long as it can keep looking at you. Then, you open the door of the cage with your hand. The dove steps forward and pops its head out, while still looking at you. Then, it takes a joyous leap forward and flies out of the cage, flexing its wings gently in the air, cherishing its newly found freedom. The dove, which represents the one you love, flies around the outside of the cage three times, with its eyes fixed on you at all times. It circles around the cage but does not want to leave you. It is free and yet it is not free.

Then, you call out to the bird and say, *"I love you enough to let you go."* Keep looking at the dove and repeat these words until it begins to fly away from you. It is now completely free.

When you love something so dearly, you must be able to let it go, for *true love only lives in freedom*. Watch your loved one fly away into the horizon and be happy for his or her freedom. Initially, you may feel a sense of loss, but soon, it will pass. Then, you may open your eyes and sit quietly for a minute, internalising the feelings of letting your loved one go.

Now, still sitting in a completely relaxed position, prepare for the final meditation.

Meditation of Reunion

When you are ready, close your eyes once again. Imagine that you are looking into the horizon. The sun is setting and the sky has turned a crimson colour. After a few moments of looking at the horizon, start repeating the words, *"Welcome back, my love."* Keep repeating these words internally, slowly and gently.

You will now see the dove appear in the horizon and it is flying towards you. Hold your arms open and keep repeating, *"Welcome back, my love."* Watch the dove flap its majestic wings as it races back towards you. When it has finally reached you, it stops, spreads both its wings wide apart and starts to ease its way slowly into your open arms. Keep repeating the welcoming words and allow the dove, with its wings wide open, to come so close to you that it finally merges into you. It is now yours, completely yours. It has merged into you. It has become you.

You can see the empty cage in front of you. Your loved one is truly free now, within you. Internalise your feelings of reunion for a minute or two as you continue to sit with your eyes closed. Repeat the *words of reaffirmation, "I love you,"* for a few more moments. When you are ready you may open your eyes.

This process of meditation is a truly beautiful experience. You begin by reaffirming your love, then you free your loved one by letting go and finally you welcome him or her back into your embrace, into a blissful reunion. Practising this meditation regularly will help you to find the fulfilment that you feel you are lacking. If your partner practises this meditation each day also, either with you, or, ideally, on his or her own, then you may find some wonderful changes beginning to take place in your relationship. Even if only one of you practises the meditation, it will still work wonders for your relationship.

These meditations are not only for lovers. They can be practised to find fulfilment that you feel is lacking in the relationship with your friends, children, parents or whomever you love dearly, because they enable you to develop a healthy detachment. This meditation is also very helpful in dealing with a loved one who is very ill and is not likely to live for long. Set them free and you will find great value in the time that remains before they depart.

CLOSING THE VOID OF REJECTION

We have talked about *love desires* that are fully or partially fulfilled. What happens when we love someone and they do not love us back? What happens if we try so hard to win the love of a man or a woman but he or she just does not respond? In these circumstances, the *love desire* can become a source of internal and external conflict. We have to learn to let go of the person whom we love, in a manner that is positive and healthy. The following meditation, which is called the *Meditation of Detachment,* will be helpful in closing the void of rejection.

Meditation of Detachment

This meditation is similar to the *Meditation of Freedom* as described earlier, with certain differences towards the end of the meditation.

Sit in a relaxed position, close your eyes and breathe freely. Imagine that you are looking at a golden birdcage that is in front of you. It is a beautiful cage with gentle, rounded edges. In this cage is a magnificent white dove that is looking through the wires of the cage at you, with warm, loving eyes. Take a few moments and look at this bird, for it is indeed a representation of your loved one.

The dove looks happy to be in its cage, as long as it can keep looking at you. Then, you open the door of the cage with your hand. The dove steps forward and pops its head out, while still looking at you. Then, it takes a joyous leap forward and flies out of the cage, flexing its wings gently in the air, cherishing its newly found freedom. The dove, which represents the one you love, flies around the outside of the cage three times, with its eyes fixed on you at all times. It circles around the cage but does not want to leave you. It is free and yet it is not free.

Then, you call out to this bird and say, *"I love you enough to let you go."* Keep looking at the dove and repeat these words until it begins to fly away from you. It is now completely free.

You can see your beloved dove fly towards the horizon, where the sun is setting. Allow the dove to completely disappear into the horizon. Now, you can see nothing but the horizon. The sun continues to set and the darkness begins to fill the sky. Soon, all you can see is darkness.

In the distance, you can see a little speck of light, like a star. It starts to grow larger as it comes towards you until it stops at a point where you can just see its contour. It is your beloved dove that has returned, but now, it is no longer white. It has turned golden and luminous, giving off a beautiful light. You cannot see its face clearly, nor can you see its eyes, because it is not close enough.

Keep looking at this light for a few moments and then repeat the words, *"I am here for you,"* internally and quietly. The bird stays where it is. It does not move, but it has received your message. Continue to repeat these words for a minute, while constantly looking at the dove.

Spend a few moments internalising your feelings about letting go of your loved one and being there for him or her, should they choose to come back to you. When you are ready, open your eyes.

The darkness that you see in your meditation, which follows the sunset, symbolises the "unknown" aspect of the outcome for your love.

The change in colour of the dove from white to golden symbolises "hope" that this light may overcome the darkness so that the dove may fly to you someday and fill you with light. On that day, there will be no more darkness.

The luminous bird standing still at a distance from you represents "patience". You are waiting for the reunion, if it is to occur. You are there for the one you love.

The *Meditation of Detachment* is a powerful method of healing the void within oneself. After performing this meditation a number of times, you will find that you will be able to detach from the one you love but who does not love you back. You may find that over time, your feelings towards the person you love may change and, because you will have detached yourself from him or her, you will have opened yourself up to the possibility of a new love relationship. The process of detaching and then opening oneself is extremely important. After some time, the pain that comes from your unfulfilled love will begin to leave you.

If you are fortunate and through your meditation you are able to draw the one you love towards you, then there will be a happy ending. If not, you will find the true happiness that you seek elsewhere.

OVERCOMING LUST DESIRES

L et us now reflect on how we can best deal with the raw, *lust desires.* Consider the following situations:

- A 16-year-old boy who has a strong desire to have sex with a beautiful 18-year-old girl.
- A 20-year-old woman who is strongly drawn sexually to a handsome, 30-year-old man.
- A 50-year-old man who has an uncontrollable desire to have sex with a gorgeous 30-year-old supermodel.
- A 45-year-old woman who has a dying urge to have sex with a handsome 22-year-old athlete.
- A 35-year-old man who is strongly attracted homosexually to an 18-year-old boy.
- A 40-year-old mother of two who is sexually obsessed with a 25-year-old woman.

Let us assume that we fit into one of the above categories. The ages and genders may vary. We feel an intense and powerful sexual *desire* towards the boy, girl, man or woman, to the point that it hurts. How do we overcome this *desire?*

The first thing we need to do is to provide an outlet for our built-up energies. We could, for example, take up sports, like swimming, jogging or any other physical activity that drains our energies. This would help to a certain extent.

Another option would be to bury ourselves in activities that distract us mentally from this powerful sexual *desire.* Such activities could include work, reading, joining clubs, taking up new responsibilities, etc. I am certain that each one of us has an interest that we can immerse ourselves in.

Finally, we could practise the following meditation, which is called the *Meditation of Familiarity*.

Meditation of Familiarity

Sit quietly and comfortably in a room, by yourself. Make sure that you are completely relaxed. Close your eyes and think about the person you are sexually attracted to. Imagine that this person is standing before you and you are completely taken in by his or her physical beauty.

Next, bring this person very close to you in spirit and in relationship. You can do this by repeating quietly to yourself, *"He/she is one of me"*. (You can insert the name of this person in place of he/she, if you wish).

Keep repeating these words as you watch the person of your desires. Your words are bringing him or her closer and closer to your soul.

Then you can start to give a "familial dimension" to this closeness. You may do this by repeating the words, *"He is my brother"* or *"She is my sister"* or *"He is my son"* or *"She is my daughter"* etc. You can choose a familial relationship that you are comfortable with. It should be a relationship that strongly repels any notion of sex in your mind.

Keep watching this person while repeating the words that make him or her a part of your family (spousal relationships should be excluded!). Continue to meditate upon this closeness until you are ready to stop.

You may open your eyes and internalise your feelings of familial closeness to the person you are sexually attracted to. As you practise this meditation regularly, you will find your sexual desire for this person extinguishing itself, step by step. When you see this person physically, think of them as the family member that you imagined in your meditation.

I am sure you will appreciate that the subject of *love* and *lust desire* is vast and cannot possibly be covered in its entirety in this short book. However, for the purposes of understanding and learning to overcome conflict, with respect to sexuality, the discussion and the meditations presented in this chapter provide useful practical tools and healthy steps in the journey towards achieving *zero conflict*.

Note: Audio cassettes and CDs of this entire book, which include the above meditations, are available separately. The meditations are presented in a manner that is easy to follow. Just sit back and listen to them as you are guided through the special learning experiences. Please visit your bookshop or www.amyndahya.com for further details.

Seeds of Resolution

✿ Let us contemplate and internalise the following seeds:

"I AM LOVE.

I AM LIGHT.

I AM EMPOWERED WITH SEXUALITY

TO BRING LIFE, SACRED AND PURE."

My Reflections

Now

date: /   /   .

My Reflections

One Year Hence   date: /   /   .

My Reflections

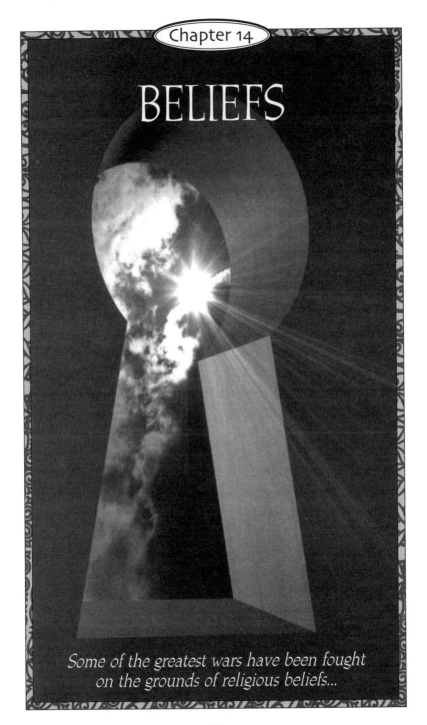

Chapter 14

BELIEFS

*Some of the greatest wars have been fought
on the grounds of religious beliefs...*

When we are born, we come into this world with pure, innocent minds. We have no biases and know no difference between right and wrong. In our little worlds, we just 'be' as we did before birth. Then, as we grow up, we develop our biases and attitudes as a result of external influences. We embrace the beliefs of those around us as our own. We then proceed to naïvely consider that whatever we believe in is correct, and anything that does not coincide with our own beliefs, is incorrect. By this time, we have long stopped living in our own innocent little worlds where we just be. We have dramatically changed them in that they now consist of new beliefs, attitudes, jealousies, likes and dislikes, etc. Our little worlds are now littered with the elements of conflict.

As we grow older, these elements become more prominent. Our personalities take on their own unique traits, as do our worlds. Because we are all interconnected, we influence the worlds of others with the elements that reside in our world. This is how we spread our own ideas, beliefs, influences and conflicts. Similarly, our own world absorbs elements from the worlds of others. This is how some people become positive influences on us, whilst others become negative influences. People who are positive influences are driven by positive motivations in their worlds. People who are negative influences are driven by negative motivations in their worlds. We all impact on one another in very significant ways each and every moment of our lives. Hence, as we move towards zero conflict, we can cause the whole world to move towards zero conflict. Each one of us is indeed very influential in this process!

In order to move towards zero conflict, we must cultivate great flexibility from within. This flexibility can be achieved if we work consciously towards it. However, one very significant impediment in this process is our beliefs — what they entail, how we deal with them, and how we express them.

We have many beliefs in virtually every area of our lives. However, in the context of achieving zero conflict, it is particularly important to examine our religious beliefs. Religious beliefs are very personal to each one of us. The word religion, in this context, is not restricted to the major religions of the world, such as, Christianity, Islam, Judaism, Buddhism, Hinduism, Taoism, etc. Religion goes beyond structured, organised ways of living and worshipping our Creator. It is actually a very personal, inner relationship that each one of us has with our Source or Origin, regardless of what name we ascribe to our Origin, or in what dimension we perceive the presence of our Origin. Common names for the Origin include God, Allah, Dios, Bhagwaan, Ishwar, Nature, etc. Those who do not believe in the concept of a Creator may call the Origin a "Statistical Coincidence!" No matter how we choose to say it, the fact of the matter is that we all come from a common Origin. This is the essence and foundation of all religions.

While religion in itself is a simple recognition of the truth about oneself and one's Origin, the external elements, such as, religious doctrines, ideologies, rituals, sectarian ideals, traditions, cults, etc., often create division, confusion and conflicts in the minds and attitudes of people who do not understand the underlying essence of all the religions. As a result, some of us grow up believing that our beliefs and notions are correct and all others are incorrect.

We must pause and ask the question, "What qualifies me to decide who is right and who is wrong about their beliefs? By what authority can I make such judgements?" Depending upon the religious doctrines we follow, some of us will attempt to answer such deep, personal questions by referencing a scripture that we believe in. Such a reference may not always be entirely correct, because if we are completely honest with ourselves, we will know that none of us is actually qualified to judge other people's religious beliefs, attitudes, way of life, or preferences. Even the scriptures that we believe in are open to infinite levels of interpretation. This is what makes them so unique. Therefore, we cannot possibly claim the authority to judge the beliefs of others on the basis of scriptures whose levels of interpretation transcend the capacity of the human mind.

Some of us are very anxious to impose our own beliefs upon others because we naïvely think that we will be helping them or saving them! As a matter of fact, if we could help ourselves and save ourselves (whatever save means), then that in itself would be a major accomplishment of a lifetime. We should realise that if we are not qualified to judge others, then we are most certainly not qualified to impose our own beliefs on others. Acceptance of religious beliefs must be an honest and a voluntary exercise, with no compulsion or fear. My comments should not be misconstrued as being against sharing the teachings of our religions and beliefs with others. Sharing knowledge is a positive exercise, as long as it is done in the absence of pressure and compulsion. True learning, especially with respect to matters of the soul, always occurs in complete freedom, since it is a very personal process.

The following story, which is an excerpt from Reflections from the Origin, provides invaluable insights into beliefs, as seen through the eyes of two birds.

THE SPARROW AND THE DOVE

It was a dark, starry night. At a family retreat in Banff, amidst the Rocky Mountains in Canada, men, women and children had gathered around a campfire to listen to the wise Herald speak. They were going to learn about God and the many different ways in which the people of the world perceive God.

The Herald started by saying, "Many a time, I have listened to conversations where people of different professions, races and interests have discussed God. In some cases, the tone of the conversation is calm and peaceful. In other cases, there are heated debates. Some challenge those who believe in God. Others argue about the very existence of God. Some with strong views ridicule others, condemning them for their difference in beliefs, and so it goes on and on... It is a debate. It is emotional, funny, fearful, scornful, sad, rational and irrational! What a debate! Who is right, and who is wrong? This is typically the issue. I wonder, why does anyone have to be right? Or, why does anyone have to be wrong? And, who is to decide between right and wrong? Are we really capable of making such a judgement? If so, on what basis, one must ask. This is another debate!"

The Herald continued, "I will relate to you a story of the sparrow and the dove, which will bring home an important message to each one of you."

There was once a sparrow that flew in the sky. It looked at the earth and only saw green fields. Then, it flew over a lake, and the earth was one solid mass of water in the eyes of this sparrow. Then, it flew over a mountain covered with snow; the world now seemed to be a sheet of plain white! Then, the sparrow flew over the desert and saw the earth as one mass of brown sand! As it flew on its journey, it saw trees, grass, water, snow, rocks, sand, rich green fields and dry brown deserts. Then, it landed on a tall baobab tree to rest. One half of the baobab tree had leaves and the other half had none! Just then, a white dove landed on the baobab tree, also to rest.

The two birds looked at each other and the sparrow asked, "Where are you heading to?"

The dove replied, "My entire life is a journey, with a destination I know not."

The sparrow then asked, "Where do you live? Above what part of the land is your home?"

The dove replied, "The land is the earth and the earth is the land — I can tell no difference."

"But," said the sparrow, "I live above the land with rich green grass — that is my home, and that is the *only* earth there is."

The dove then asked, "Have you ever flown over the glittering land which sparkles in the sunshine and looks deep and lonely in the darkness? And when the wind blows, this land has ripples and waves — sometimes it rages with waves and splashes all around?"

The sparrow replied, "Of course I have flown over that glittering land, but that is not the earth! I once tried to step on it, but the land was false. I could not set my feet on this glittering land, because each time I tried, the land opened up and in went my feet! My dear dove, that is a false land, and it is not the earth for sure!"

The dove then asked, "Have you ever flown over the brown sands that blaze in the heat?"

The sparrow had a frown on its face. "Of course, I have seen those strange lands. Each time I set foot on the brown land, I jumped up because my feet kept getting burnt. Like the false land that parted each time I set foot on it, these sands too are not the earth because all they do is burn my feet! And, I can assure you, these sands are *not* the earth!"

The dove then remarked, "You must have flown over the land that almost touches the sky?"

The sparrow had a smile on its face. "Yes, but that land too is false because when I look at it from afar, it is touching the sky. But, when I fly over it, the sky is a long, long way away! Once I tried to set foot on the white fluff (snow) that grows on top of this land, and it felt very strange! I felt the same pain as I did when I tried to stand on the brown sand. But, whilst the pain felt the same, it was still different. I think this land never tells the truth. It looks different to me every time I look at it, from afar and from close by. That could never be a home for anybody; that could *never* be the earth!"

By this time, the dove was quite amused. The sparrow seemed to have seen the different lands, but only *its* home was the earth! Everything else was false or strange! The dove then asked the sparrow, "What if I were to say that all the lands that you saw are the earth?"

The sparrow replied, "With due respect, my dear dove, I would have to say that you are mad — only a mad bird could say something so absurd! There is only one earth, and that is where the rich green grass grows. Everything else is false!"

The dove then said, "All the lands we talked about — the glittering land, the burning sands, the white fluff — are they not all 'lands,' for that is what you have called them all along?"

"Yes," replied the sparrow. "But they are all very different and so they are false!"

The dove then said, "My dear sparrow, you agree that all these false places are 'lands,' but since they behave strangely to you, you cannot understand them. But, they are all 'lands.' Suppose I were to say that they are one 'land' with differences?"

The sparrow seemed to get very flustered. "You cannot have all these strange 'lands' in one 'land'! The only land that I think is real is the green land where I live, and that, my dear friend, is the 'earth.' I know this for sure because I live there. It is as real as real can be, and everything else is false!"

The dove could see that although the sparrow had seen much, it understood little. Here was a bird that had travelled far and wide, and seen lands that were so different. Yet, the green field was the only reality it knew. The dove, being a wise bird, asked the sparrow, "Would you say that we are both standing on a baobab tree?"

To that the sparrow replied, "Of course. We are here, aren't we?"

The dove then said, "Would you say that this tree has leaves?" The sparrow replied, "Of course. Are you blind?"

The dove flapped its wings and said, "Look behind you. Do you see any leaves on that half of the tree?"

The sparrow replied, "No, there are no leaves on that part of the tree, but it is a baobab tree. I know because I am standing on it!"

The dove smiled and said, "So you agree that it is a tree that we are standing on?"

"Of course!" replied the sparrow.

"But one half of the tree is so different from the other. So, why don't we say that this tree is in fact two different trees?"

The sparrow looked confused and said, "You have a point, but this is one tree, I can assure you!"

The dove the asked, "Just as the baobab tree embodies such remarkable differences within itself, why can't the 'different lands' be just one 'land'? And this one 'land' be the 'earth'?"

The sparrow had a twinkle in its eye. It said, "I guess you have a point. You may have sold me on the 'tree' story, but the 'earth' is a whole different matter. *I guess you doves really need to be sparrows to know what the 'earth' is!*"

All the eyes around the campfire were fixed on the Herald. There was pin-drop silence and it was clear that the audience wanted to hear more.

The Herald continued, "In every debate about God, there are sparrows and doves. In fact, the very idea that God exists is difficult for some to understand. And then, there are some who consider their religion and perception of God as being the only "true path" — just like the sparrow and the green field. Then, there are others who view God through the physical things that surround them. Some view God in a spiritual context. Some atheists, or those who do not comprehend God, say that what we call 'God' is just a form of 'Energy.' We all describe God in so many different ways."

A 14-year-old boy, who had listened to the Herald with great interest asked, "How many different Gods are there and which one of the two birds was correct?"

The Herald replied, "The truth about the existence of all living things is that there is only one common Origin, from where we draw our energies of life and all our resources. When you think of the sparrow and the dove, both birds flew over the same lands and yet each one of them interpreted what they saw in a completely different manner. The sparrow in its own right was correct in what it saw and felt. But then, so was the dove.

The Herald continued, "When we think of God — that very thought alone is wonderful. And when we talk about our beliefs or opinions, we must remember the sparrow and the dove, for there is no wrong and no right! Why should anyone be 'wrong' in his or her perception of God? And, why should anyone be 'right' about God? Who can judge between the right and the wrong?"

He chuckled and then said, "God only knows!"

It was now time for the children to go to bed, although they would all rather have stayed up and listened to the Herald. He concluded by saying, "Good night to you all, my dear ones. Remember that if anyone should ever suggest that their view of God is the only correct one, and that everything else is false, then they may have been spending too much time with the sparrow! You may want to suggest the broader perspective of the dove. But even that may be nowhere near broad enough!"

Everyone laughed at that remark and then got up to return to their log cabins. The little children flapped their hands, imagining that they were birds. They split into two groups; one called themselves the sparrows and the other, the doves. Even though what the Herald had shared with them was a simple and a funny story, some permanent seeds had been planted in their young minds that would one day bear fruits of peace and acceptance.

A careful look at history will reveal that, some of the greatest wars have been fought on the grounds of religious beliefs. They have been a major source of conflict, typically expressed through social, political or personal perspectives. Yet, the essence of religion, in itself, is inherently simple and peaceful. Therefore, if we are to move *towards zero conflict*, we need to focus our attention particularly on the essence that underlies our religious beliefs. We need to recognise that this essence is common to all beliefs. Hence, essence unites us all into Oneness.

Our religious beliefs should be based upon complete flexibility. We should cherish our own essence and respect the fact that the very same essence is present in all those around us. In this way, we will learn *'religious acceptance'*, which is crucial to achieving *zero conflict*. I do not subscribe to the term *'religious tolerance'*, because the word *tolerance* is still divisive. The word *acceptance* is uniting and enables us to freely embrace each other through recognition of the common essence that binds us together, as one humanity. In this way, we can all happily practise our own religions, in whatever way we choose, whilst fully accepting the views and ways of our fellow beings at all times.

Let us conclude with the simple understanding that we all come from one Source. There is one super-highway that leads us all to that Source. This highway is comprised of many lanes. Think of each religion as simply a lane in this beautiful highway. It does not matter which lane we travel in. What matters is that we accept the fact that all the lanes make up this highway, which leads us all to one destination, our Origin.

Seeds of Resolution

❀ Let us contemplate and internalise the following seeds:

"I AM ESSENCE
FREE AND PURE.
I SEE ESSENCE IN ALL
FOR I AM ALL."

My Reflections

Now

date: / / .

244

My Reflections

One Year Hence   date: /   /   .

My Reflections

Chapter 15

INTERNALISATION AND TESTING OF FEELINGS

"Knowing our feelings helps us to manage them better"

In the preceding chapters, we examined the various types of conflicts that cause us and others pain, frustration and unhappiness. We also looked at ways of understanding the sources of the conflicts and methods of dealing with them. Conflicts often manifest as deep emotions, which can leave long-lasting scars within us.

Clearly, if we are to take positive strides towards zero conflict, we must first be able to heal ourselves from within. We must be able to let go of our hurts, pains, anger and frustrations. We must be able to release the thoughts and feelings that have inflicted us with such deep scars.

The following is an exercise to determine how each of us experiences and internalises our feelings:

Testing our Feelings

The object of this exercise is to evoke some feelings within you in order to identify the part(s) of your body that are impacted by these feelings, and to evaluate the time-frames over which you typically carry these feelings. Write down your answer to each of the questions and make a mark on the diagram at the exact spot where you experience the emotions, mark your positive and negative feelings with different symbols or colours, so that you can clearly differentiate between them. If there is no single spot in your body where these feelings manifest, then shade the entire diagram with a pencil, indicating that your feelings are being experienced throughout the body. Take your time and give detailed answers, expressing clearly all the emotions that you experience. Be completely honest with yourself. Fully answer each question before proceeding to the next one.

Space has been provided for you to conduct the same exercise one year from now, so that you can evaluate the changes that you have undergone as a result of practising the lessons in this book (if you have indeed done so).

1 *You are sitting in your living room listening to your father tell you off about how irresponsible you have been. You are told that you are not capable of completing any task without*

Now

a) How do you feel?

_____

_____

_____

b) Please locate the point or points in your body where these feelings manifest, in the following diagram.

c) How long are you going to remember this event?

_____

_____

d)How does this make you feel about your sibling?

_____

_____

e)How does it make you feel about your father?

_____

_____

messing things up. You are told that you can never be as good as your sibling. There is much that you want to say in your defence but you are not given the opportunity to do so.

ONE YEAR FROM NOW

a) How do you feel?

b) Please locate the point or points in your body where these feelings manifest, in the following diagram.

c) How long are you going to remember this event?

d)How does this make you feel about your sibling?

e)How does it make you feel about your father?

2 *You are sitting in your office looking at your payslip. After all the deductions, you are left with barely enough to get by. Then, you see a headline on a newspaper on your desk, which catches your eye. The article is about your classmate, who*

NOW

a) How do you feel?

b) Please locate the point or points in your body where these feelings manifest, in the following diagram.

c) How long are you going to remember this event?

d) How do you feel about your classmate?

e) Would you like to see him become even more successful?

d) Or would you like to see him fall?

was once your rival at school, having become a successful millionaire. He is due to receive an award of excellence from the Governor.

ONE YEAR FROM NOW

a) How do you feel?

b) Please locate the point or points in your body where these feelings manifest, in the following diagram.

c) How long are you going to remember this event?

d) How do you feel about your classmate?

e) Would you like to see him ecome even more successful?

d) Or would you like to see him fall?

3 *Then, you turn another page of the newspaper and you read about how 50 people lost their jobs when a factory in your area closed down. Of these, five people were your classmates.*

NOW

a) How do you feel about them?

_____

_____

b) How do you feel about yourself?

_____

c) Please locate the point or points in your body where these feelings manifest, in the following diagram.

d) How long are you going to remember this event?

_____

e)How do you feel about your millionaire classmate now?

_____

f)Please locate the point or points in your body where these feelings now manifest, in the above diagram.

_____

ONE YEAR FROM NOW

a) How do you feel about them?

b) How do you feel about yourself?

c) Please locate the point or points in your body where these feelings manifest, in the following diagram.

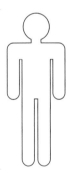

d) How long are you going to remember this event?

e)How do you feel about your millionaire classmate now?

f)Please locate the point or points in your body where these feelings now manifest, in the above diagram.

4 *You are at your high school dance and the girl you absolutely adore has come to the dance with someone else. She does not even notice your presence. She is completely*

Now

a) How do you feel?

_____

_____

_____

_____

b) Please locate the point or points in your body where these feelings manifest, in the following diagram.

c) How long are you going to remember this event?

_____

_____

_____

d) How does this make you feel about the person he (or she) is with?

_____

_____

_____

_____

engrossed in the person she is dancing with. (Please reverse the genders as appropriate).

ONE YEAR FROM NOW

a) How do you feel?

_____

_____

_____

b) Please locate the point or points in your body where these feelings manifest, in the following diagram.

c) How long are you going to remember this event?

_____

_____

_____

d) How does this make you feel about the person he (or she) is with?

_____

_____

_____

_____

5 *You are in your final year at college. You go to a farewell dance where you come face-to-face with the boy of your dreams. He looks at you and asks you to dance with him.*

Now

a) How do you feel?

_____

_____

_____

_____

b) Please locate the point or points in your body where these feelings manifest, in the following diagram.

c) How long are you going to remember this event?

_____

_____

_____

d)What parts of the evening's experience are you likely to remember the most?

_____

_____

_____

_____

You spend the evening with him and learn that he cares about you as much as you care about him. (Please reverse the genders as appropriate).

ONE YEAR FROM NOW

a) How do you feel?

b) Please locate the point or points in your body where these feelings manifest, in the following diagram.

c) How long are you going to remember this event?

d)What parts of the evening's experience are you likely to remember the most?

6 *Your closest friend comes to you in desperate need of $5,000. You have no spare money but you go out of your way to help her and borrow it on your credit card. She promises to pay you back by the time your credit card statement arrives. She fails to do so*

NOW

a) How do you feel?

b) Please locate the point or points in your body where these feelings manifest, in the following diagram.

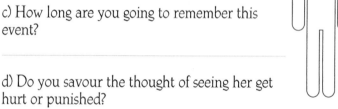

c) How long are you going to remember this event?

d) Do you savour the thought of seeing her get hurt or punished?

e) If you had an opportunity to expose her indiscretion to the public, would you do so?

f) If your answer is yes, and assuming that you have actually proceeded to expose her, how do you feel now? Did the revenge feel good?

g) Where does this feeling now reside in your body and how long will you remember this event?

and starts to avoid you. She dodges you each time you try to approach her. This goes on for six months, then, she stops talking to you. You are left in a difficult position financially. (Please reverse the genders as appropriate).

ONE YEAR FROM NOW

a) How do you feel?

b) Please locate the point or points in your body where these feelings manifest, in the following diagram.

c) How long are you going to remember this event?

d) Do you savour the thought of seeing her get hurt or punished?

e) If you had an opportunity to expose her indiscretion to the public, would you do so?

f) If your answer is yes, and assuming that you have actually proceeded to expose her, how do you feel now? Did the revenge feel good?

g) Where does this feeling now reside in your body and how long will you remember this event?

7 *You love your wife very much and one day you find out that she has been having an affair with your best friend. You learn that this affair has been going on for five years.*

Now

a) How do you feel about her now?

b) Please locate the point or points in your body where these feelings manifest, in the following diagram.

c) How long are you going to remember this event?

d) How do you feel about your best friend?

e) Do these feelings rest in the same spot within your body or do they rest in different places? If so, where?

f) Would you consider revenge, and if so, what would you do?

g) Would you consider the possibility that you may have had a part to play in her indiscretion? If so, how do you feel when you realise that you may have been the cause of this distressful situation? Where does this feeling reside in your body?

You confront her about it and she admits it to you. She begs your forgiveness and promises never to be unfaithful to you again. (Please reverse the genders as appropriate).

ONE YEAR FROM NOW

a) How do you feel about her now?

b) Please locate the point or points in your body where these feelings manifest, in the following diagram.

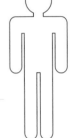

c) How long are you going to remember this event?

d) How do you feel about your best friend?

e)Do these feelings rest in the same spot within your body or do they rest in different places? If so, where?

f)Would you consider revenge, and if so, what would you do?

g)Would you consider the possibility that you may have had a part to play in her indiscretion? If so, how do you feel when you realise that you may have been the cause of this distressful situation? Where does this feeling reside in your body?

8 *You are a financial controller of a company and during your difficult times, you borrowed $10,000 from the company without anyone's knowledge. You planned to* return the money as soon as you could. An associate finds out

Now

a) How do you feel about:
   * your superior finding out

   * going to jail

   * the person who is blackmailing you

b) Where does each of these feelings reside in you? Do they all reside at the same place or are they at different spots?

c) How long are you going to remember this event?

d) Given the opportunity, would you try to get back at your blackmailer in the future?

e) If the answer is yes, and assuming you have been successful, how does it feel, and where does the feeling reside in your body?

what you have done. She threatens to report this to your superior or take the matter to the police, unless you pay her $1,000 every month from your monthly salary of $3,000.

ONE YEAR FROM NOW

a) How do you feel about:
   * your superior finding out

   * going to jail

   * the person who is blackmailing you

b) Where does each of these feelings reside in you? Do they all reside at the same place or are they at different spots?

c) How long are you going to remember this event?

d) Given the opportunity, would you try to get back at your blackmailer in the future?

e) If the answer is yes, and assuming you have been successful, how does it feel, and where does the feeling reside in your body?

9

You have bought a lottery ticket with a $10 million prize. You need to match eight numbers. Seven out of the eight numbers match, but you miss the jackpot by one number.

Now

a) How do you fee?

_____

_____

b) Please locate the point or points in your body where these feelings manifest, in the following diagram.

c) How long are you going to remember this event?

d) Would this experience make you feel like an unlucky person always?

_____

_____

e) Or will you remember and be grateful for the good things that have happened in your life thus far?

_____

_____

ONE YEAR FROM NOW

a) How do you fee?

_____

_____

_____

b) Please locate the point or points in your body where these feelings manifest, in the following diagram.

c) How long are you going to remember this event?

_____

d) Would this experience make you feel like an unlucky person always?

_____

_____

e) Or will you remember and be grateful for the good things that have happened in your life thus far?

_____

_____

_____

10

You later find that you had made a mistake and that all your eight numbers have matched to give you the jackpot prize of $10 million.

Now

a) How do you feel?

_____

_____

_____

b) Please locate the point or points in your body where these feelings manifest, in the following diagram.

c) How long are you going to remember this event?

d) Would this experience make you feel like a lucky person always?

_____

_____

_____

e) Or will you remember the times in your life when you have not been so lucky?

_____

_____

_____

ONE YEAR FROM NOW

a) How do you feel?

b) Please locate the point or points in your body where these feelings manifest, in the following diagram.

c) How long are you going to remember this event?

d) Would this experience make you feel like a lucky person always?

e)Or will you remember the times in your life when you have not been so lucky?

11

You are an attractive woman who has just been attacked sexually by a man who is much bigger and stronger than you. You fought hard to keep him off you but after a

NOW

a) How do you feel?

b) Please locate the point or points in your body where these feelings manifest, in the following diagram.

c) How long are you going to remember this event?

d) Would you hurt this man if you had an opportunity to do so in the future?

e) How do you feel about the people who failed to come to your rescue?

f) Where do your feelings towards them reside?

g) Would you rescue someone that was facing the same plight as you even if it was dangerous to do so?

while, you had to give in. Nobody came to your rescue because they were too afraid or they didn't care. (Please reverse the genders as appropriate).

ONE YEAR FROM NOW

a) How do you feel?

b) Please locate the point or points in your body where these feelings manifest, in the following diagram.

c) How long are you going to remember this event?

d) Would you hurt this man if you had an opportunity to do so in the future?

e) How do you feel about the people who failed to come to your rescue?

f) Where do your feelings towards them reside?

g) Would you rescue someone that was facing the same plight as you even if it was dangerous to do so?

12 *Your best friend and you belong to the same faith and you pray together often and participate in religious festivals as a team. Then, one day you*

Now

a) How do you feel about this?

b) Please locate the point or points in your body where these feelings manifest, in the following diagram.

c) How long are you going to remember this event?

d) Are you going to try to convert him or her back to your faith?

e) If so, on what basis do you plan to do this?

f) Would you try to learn more about and understand the new faith that your friend has embraced?

g) How do you feel about this new faith and its followers?

h) Where do these feelings reside in your body?

discover that he or she has given up the faith and converted to another religion.

ONE YEAR FROM NOW

a) How do you feel about this?

b) Please locate the point or points in your body where these feelings manifest, in the following diagram.

c) How long are you going to remember this event?

d) Are you going to try to convert him or her back to your faith?

e) If so, on what basis do you plan to do this?

f) Would you try to learn more about and understand the new faith that your friend has embraced?

g) How do you feel about this new faith and its followers?

h) Where do these feelings reside in your body?

13

Instead of your friend in the previous question, let us assume that it is your own child who has given up the faith to join another.

NOW

a) How do you feel about this now?

b) Please locate the point or points in your body where these feelings manifest, in the following diagram.

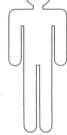

c) How long are you going to remember this event?

d) Are you going to try to convert him or her back to your faith?

e) If so, on what basis do you plan to do this?

f) Would you try to learn about and understand the new faith that your child has embraced?

g) How do you feel about this new faith and its followers?

h)Where do these feelings reside in your body?

ONE YEAR FROM NOW

a) How do you feel about this now?

b) Please locate the point or points in your body where these feelings manifest, in the following diagram.

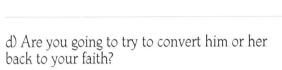

c) How long are you going to remember this event?

d) Are you going to try to convert him or her back to your faith?

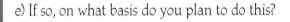

e) If so, on what basis do you plan to do this?

f) Would you try to learn about and understand the new faith that your child has embraced?

g) How do you feel about this new faith and its followers?

h) Where do these feelings reside in your body?

14

You have just read in the newspaper that your best childhood friend and one time business partner has been sued for fraud by a major corporation, who accuses your friend of committing crimes beyond your imagination. Witnesses have been produced to

Now

a) How do you feel about your friend?

b) Please locate the point or points in your body where these feelings manifest, in the following diagram.

c) How long are you going to remember this event?

d) Would you believe what the newspapers say?

f) Would you call your friend and offer your help?

g) Or would you keep as far away from your friend as possible for fear that you may become guilty by association?

h) If you chose to keep away, how do you feel about this?

substantiate the allegations against your friend. The press is in a complete frenzy over this and wherever you go, this is all you hear about. Yet, the person you are reading about is very different to the person you knew.

ONE YEAR FROM NOW

a) How do you feel about your friend?

b) Please locate the point or points in your body where these feelings manifest, in the following diagram.

c) How long are you going to remember this event?

d) Would you believe what the newspapers say?

f) Would you call your friend and offer your help?

g) Or would you keep as far away from your friend as possible for fear that you may become guilty by association?

h) If you chose to keep away, how do you feel about this?

15

If the roles were reversed and you were the accused, would your friend have believed in you and stood by you?

Now

a) If the answer is yes, how would this make you feel?

_____

_____

_____

b) Please locate the point or points in your body where these feelings manifest, in the following diagram.

c) How long are you going to remember this event?

_____

d) If your friend had chosen to keep away from you, how would you feel, especially if you were innocent?

_____

_____

_____

e) Where would these feelings reside and how long would you remember this experience?

_____

_____

ONE YEAR FROM NOW

a) If the answer is yes, how would this make you feel?

b) Please locate the point or points in your body where these feelings manifest, in the following diagram.

c) How long are you going to remember this event?

d) If your friend had chosen to keep away from you, how would you feel, especially if you were innocent?

e) Where would these feelings reside and how long would you remember this experience?

16

Then, one day, many months later, you read in the newspaper that the courts have pronounced your friend innocent. All the accusations against him or her

NOW

a) How does this make you feel if you had judged that your friend was guilty?

_____

_____

b) Please locate the point or points in your body where these feelings manifest, in the following diagram.

c) How long are you going to remember this event?

d) On the other hand, how does this make you feel if you had believed that your friend was innocent all along?

_____

_____

_____

e) Where would this feeling reside and how long would you remember this experience?

_____

_____

have been dropped as they were fabricated and the witnesses were either paid or extorted into submitting false testimony.

ONE YEAR FROM NOW

a) How does this make you feel if you had judged that your friend was guilty?

b) Please locate the point or points in your body where these feelings manifest, in the following diagram.

c) How long are you going to remember this event?

d) On the other hand, how does this make you feel if you had believed that your friend was innocent all along?

e) Where would this feeling reside and how long would you remember this experience?

17

You have practiced for two years, day in and day out for the national 100 metre sprint competition. On the day of the race, you are well prepared but nervous. When the race starts, you muster every ounce of energy that you have

NOW

a) How do you feel?

_____

b) Please locate the point or points in your body where these feelings manifest, in the following diagram.

c) How long are you going to remember this event?

d) Can you recall your nervous feelings before the race?

e) If yes, what were the thoughts that went through your mind at the time?

f) Please locate the point or points in your body where your nervous feelings manifested.

and run as fast as you can. You finish first. You have won the gold medal and have broken a new national record. The crowd cheers you with a standing ovation.

ONE YEAR FROM NOW

a) How do you feel?

b) Please locate the point or points in your body where these feelings manifest, in the following diagram.

c) How long are you going to remember this event?

d) Can you recall your nervous feelings before the race?

e) If yes, what were the thoughts that went through your mind at the time?

f) Please locate the point or points in your body where your nervous feelings manifested.

18

You attend a live concert, where your favourite singer is performing. Towards the end of the concert, he/she sings your favourite song, amidst a background of

Now

a) How do you feel?

b) Please locate the point or points in your body where these feelings manifest, in the following diagram.

c) How long are you going to remember this event?

d) A month after the concert, when you remember your favourite singer, how do you feel?

powerful music, which you adore. Everyone around you is singing aloud and the concert hall is filled with energy and vibrancy.

ONE YEAR FROM NOW

a) How do you feel?

b) Please locate the point or points in your body where these feelings manifest, in the following diagram.

c) How long are you going to remember this event?

d) A month after the concert, when you remember your favourite singer, how do you feel?

The above questions evoke different types of feelings within us. The object of the exercise was for us to sense these feelings and identify the areas in our body where these feelings reside. This process is called 'internalisation'. We all internalise our feelings differently. We store our emotions, pleasant or painful, within our body. Different people store their painful stresses in different parts of their bodies. Often, these stresses manifest as illnesses. The fact is that we all experience our feelings, internalise them and then store them. Depending upon the feelings, we may store them for a short time or for a very long time. The really deep feelings leave permanent scars within us.

REVIEWING YOUR ANSWERS

Take some time to carefully study all the diagrams in questions 1 to 18. Identify the parts of the body where you stored the feelings arising from each painful experience versus each pleasant one. Now mark all the areas where you stored your painful experiences in questions 1 to 18, in the diagram next page.

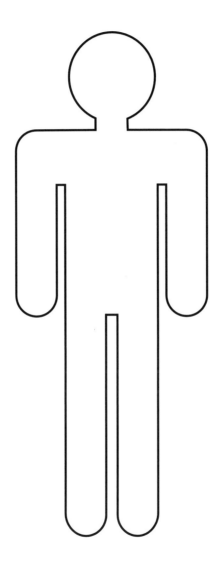

Summary of Negative Experience Locations

The above summary reveals the areas in your body that are most vulnerable to stress related illnesses. The concentration of feelings arising from painful experiences damages our organs as well as weakens the areas where they manifest. If you are already suffering from health disorders in the areas you have identified above, then you may now be able to better understand the root cause of your problems. If you are not suffering from any disorders in these areas, then it would be wise to guard against future illnesses. The practical meditations presented later in this chapter will serve as useful tools to overcome the impact of stress related damage that you may have suffered, and to provide protection against future health disorders.

You may now mark all the areas where you stored the feelings arising from your happy and fulfilling experiences in questions 1 to 18, in the diagram next page.

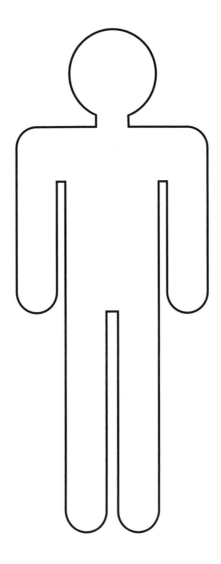

Summary of Positive Experience Locations

The above diagram reveals how you manage and internalise positive feelings that arise from happy and fulfilling experiences. It is important to note that such positive feelings often help to neutralise the damage that is cause by the negative ones. Therefore, you should always attempt to derive the most from your positive experiences. It is healthy to bask in the sunshine of your happiness!

Some people experience happy feelings throughout the body, rather than in one particular area. Such people generally tend to have a good balance between their material and spiritual lives. They allocate sufficient time and attention to their material well being, as well as their spiritual development. The term 'spiritual development' need not be restricted to the practise of one's faith. In fact, spiritual development comes from being aware of, and communicating with, one's Higher Self. In contrast, some people concentrate their happy and positive feelings in specific areas of their body. Such people generally have a weaker balance between their spiritual and material lives. Remember that we are talking about a balance that needs to exist between two very important aspects of our lives. Over-indulgence in any one aspect weakens this crucial balance.

Whilst the observations and possible interpretations from the above exercises should not be used to draw hard and fast conclusions, they can certainly serve as helpful beacons towards positive personal development. Several chapters in this book, as well as other books that I have written, provide useful guidance on creation of a balance between our material and spiritual lives.

You should now go back to the answers to each question and reflect carefully upon what you have written. Your answers, if honestly recorded, will reveal your actual inner feelings and attitudes. They will help you to identify the different types of conflicts that you harbour, as well as the damaging attitudes that you may possess. They can also help to explain the causes of some of the difficulties you may be facing in your relationships. As mentioned earlier, identifying and understanding your conflicts takes you a long way towards overcoming them.

Whilst experiences bring us learning, the depth and breadth of our feelings also grows continually each day. You should now go back to your answers once again and make note of how long you said you would remember each one of the feelings invoked by the questions. Imagine that you were to place all such feelings into a suitcase, every day of your life. You can now see how big this suitcase is going to be, especially if you think about all the feelings you have harboured since childhood! If you are the type of person who holds your feelings for a long time, then you are clearly burdening yourself with a huge amount of unnecessary baggage, which only adds to your physical, mental and emotional health issues, and saps your happiness. This is precisely why, it is essential for us to regularly clean out this suitcase by letting go of our harboured feelings. The meditations which follow in this chapter provide useful tools in this regard.

I recommend that you revisit the questions, answers and diagrams in this chapter after one year, in order to assess your evolution in the direction *towards zero conflict*. To do this, you should answer all the questions once again and add any new feelings and their locations within your body in the appropriate diagrams, so that you can observe the changes that may have taken place in your personal attitudes, behaviour and outlook towards life.

LETTING GO OF EMOTIONS

Learning to avoid accumulation of stressful feelings, and purging them out of our system, is an integral part of the healing process of our inner selves. The key is to be able to *let go* of our feelings. This is not always easy. However, the following tips may help you to get started:

1. Identify the feeling and be aware of it.
2. Ask yourself why you are feeling this way and seek to understand the motivation that is driving this feeling.
3. Try to change the motivation so that the feeling ceases to manifest.
4. If you cannot change the motivation, then allow the feeling to take its course and work towards letting it go. It should not be allowed to leave a scar within you.

Of course, the golden question is how can one *let go*? This is where all the lessons described thus far in this book become very useful. By understanding conflict and its sources, we can take significant strides towards eliminating the stressful feelings at their source. Another very useful way of letting go of the painful feelings and emotions is through a meditation called *Inner Cleansing*.

Meditation of Inner Cleansing

This meditation can be practised at any time, as long as you are in a quiet, comfortable setting. Make sure you are sitting or lying in a position where you are 100 percent comfortable. Relax yourself and breathe freely.

Now close your eyes and imagine:

You are in a small, dark room. It is very, very dark. See the darkness and feel it for a minute or so.

You are very uncomfortable in this dark room. You do not like it at all. Imagine this discomfort and feel it for a few moments.

Then, think about the issue that is causing you feelings of pain, anger, or frustration. Focus on this issue and feel the frustrations. Allow these feelings to leave your body and to fill up the dark room.

Now you are all alone in this small, dark room, surrounded by your feelings of anger, hurt, pain and frustration. Take a few moments to experience these feelings.

Now, imagine that your hands are groping against the walls of this dark room. Suddenly, you push against a window and it starts to open. Outside of this window, there is a beautiful, warm, peaceful and loving Light.

As the window opens, this Light begins to come towards you. But, it cannot enter the dark room as long as your feelings of frustration and pain are present.

So, you take a broom and start to sweep these feelings out of the window. As each feeling leaves, a beautiful, bright, warm ray of Light replaces it.

You keep sweeping these feelings out. You tell them *"It's time to go. I have no room for you in me".*

You keep sweeping them out and as they leave, you welcome the warm, beautiful Light that fills up the room.

Now, you have said goodbye to all your pain, anger and frustration. They are gone. The room is full of Light. Look at this Light. Feel it, experience it.

There is no more room for darkness in you. You only have room for Light, nothing but Light.

Keep looking at this beautiful Light and savour it for as long as you wish.

When you are ready you may open your eyes.

By using this meditation, with practice, you will feel calm, peaceful and light. Practise this meditation as frequently as you wish. In fact, each time you feel uptight and unhappy at the end of the day, take a few moments and perform Inner Cleansing. Remember, you must be in a calm, peaceful setting with no distractions in order to achieve the most from your meditation.

If you wish to be guided through this meditation, an audio tape and CD is available. Listening to the tape or CD and following the voice instructions as you meditate, will help a great deal. From experience, I have found that many people are able to concentrate better with the help of the tape or CD at the beginning. Later, they are able to perform the *Inner Cleansing* meditation very easily by themselves, without any audio assistance.

Letting go of our feelings is a powerful way of healing ourselves from within. This process also improves our physical and mental health because we are able to expel the emotions that damage our organs. How can our stresses do any damage if we do not allow them to stay within us? This inner healing process will help us to take important strides *towards zero conflict.*

Seeds of Resolution

✿ Let us contemplate and internalise the following seeds:

"I AM FREE.

I HARBOUR NO PAINS.

I HOLD NO FRUSTRATIONS.

I LET THEM GO

WITH THE WINDS THAT BLOW

FEELING THEIR FLAMES AS THEY COME AND GO

LETTING THEM NOT REST WITH ME

FOR EVEN ONE MOMENT."

My Reflections

Now   date: /   /   .

My Reflections

One Year Hence   date: /   /   .

Chapter 16

ONENESS

Human existence occurs as a combination of three states, namely body, mind and life energy. We have discussed zero conflict in some depth thus far, particularly with respect to attitudes, feelings and emotions. In order to complete the picture, we need to look at the life energy, for it is this energy that defines us as beings and embodies all the forces that keep us alive. Different cultures and religions refer to life energy in different ways. Typical names for this energy are Soul, Spirit, Alma, Aatma, Light, Nature, etc. Some even refer to this energy and it's Source as a Statistical Coincidence. I prefer to call this energy 'Ziraat', which is a neutral, universal name that does not have any affiliations with any religious ideologies, cultural practices or superstitious traditions. In essence, Ziraat can be likened to an umbilical cord that connects us to the Source from where we draw our life energy, intellect, inspirations, resources and all the tools that that we require to enable us to achieve successful accomplishment of the purpose of our life.

On April 15, 1995, I wrote about a mystical journey, called the "Sixty-Six Steps," which was later published in Reflections from the Origin. This journey had a profound impact on me and I wish to share excerpts of this experience with you, because it offers a deeper understanding of life and its purpose.

THE SIXTY-SIX STEPS
A Mystical Journey of Ascension...

I walked down the streets of an old Arabian town, watching the little children play at the doorsteps of their homes. The buildings were several hundreds of years old. The narrow streets allowed for only pedestrian traffic and possibly horse carts. After walking a long distance I stopped at a building whose facade was greyish-black from age. The written numbers on the door had faded and a rusted metal ring hung in the centre, which I presumed at some time had been used by visitors to announce their presence. Cobwebs blanketed the entire doorframe. It seemed as though no one had entered this building in centuries. I felt a strange sense of familiarity about this place though. Perhaps I had been here before. Then, suddenly, there was a deep silence in the air and the more I looked at this building, the greater my nostalgia grew. "What is it about this place?" I asked myself.

I gently pushed at the door, and to my surprise, it creaked open! I could have sworn that it was bolted shut. I pushed the door wide open and stepped into this mysterious building. Ahead of me was a staircase that seemed to go on forever. The steps were made of stone that showed the signs of their age. Each step was uneven and looked as if it had been climbed upon by millions of feet. I moved closer to the staircase and as I looked at the steps again, I saw shadow-like images of feet that had come from places far and wide. There were feet of children, of strong youths, of the middle-aged, and of the aged. These feet belonged to people of all races of this world, black, brown, white, and all shades in between! My eyes worked their way up this staircase.

It was endless! "Where did it lead? And why had all these people of great diversity tried to climb these ancient steps?" I asked myself.

From the bottom of the staircase, I carefully counted the steps. There were 66. At the 66th step, everything turned pitch dark. Something inside me kept urging me not to climb them, but rather to get out of this strange place and run for my life. The eeriness made me very uncomfortable. Yet another part of me wanted to climb up these stairs to seek out the mysteries that lay ahead. I stood still in my moments of indecision.

A cool breeze began to blow by me, and I began to hear the sounds of a crowded marketplace. I could hear voices of children, men, women, animals and all the lively spirits that existed in this marketplace. The sounds did not come from ahead of me, where the darkness lay. Rather, they seemed to come from within the walls that flanked this staircase. "What on earth is going on here?" I thought. "Who are these people that I can hear, but not see?"

I built up my courage and decided to climb this mysterious staircase. As soon as I set foot on the first step, everything went silent. I could not hear a single soul anymore. The marketplace had ceased to exist. I was not sure that I wanted to go any further! "Could I ever get out of this place alive?" I wondered. But then, almost by magic, my right foot lifted itself and made me climb up the next step, and my left foot the one after. I was now on the *third* step. Then, I heard another strange sound that also seemed to come from the walls. It was the sound of water, dripping from a tap into a pail of some sort. The water seemed to drip with regular frequency. "Where on earth is this tap?" I asked myself. I looked up the staircase and decided to count the steps again, just in case something had changed. Interestingly, from the *third* step, I could still count 66 steps ahead of me before the pitch darkness took over!

Once again, I began to climb the steps almost involuntarily. It was as if someone was guiding me up this mysterious staircase. I climbed three more steps. The sound of the dripping water had stopped. As I stood on the *sixth* step, I heard the clear ticking of a large clock that seemed to be coming through the wall. It must have been a huge grandfather clock. It ticked away with amazing precision.

I then climbed three more steps to the *ninth* step. The clock had stopped ticking, but now I could hear a beautiful sound of children frolicking in a playground. They laughed and screamed as they joyfully played a game that I could not quite recognise. There must have been 10 to 15 children. I counted the steps that lay ahead of me and there were still 66.

As I climbed up three more steps to the *twelfth* step, the voices of the children in the playground vanished. I was now getting used to the sudden changes in audio-scenery! On the *twelfth* step, I heard the refreshing sound of a waterfall. It was as if I was standing in the middle of a 100-foot waterfall, which I could not see. And still, ahead of me lay 66 steps.

I looked behind me and was amazed to see that the darkness had formed a wall! I could not even see one step back. I was trapped by the darkness, which now existed behind me and at the dark curtain that stood ahead of me, 66 steps away. However, I was no longer afraid. Rather, I was quite curious to unravel the mystery behind this unusual staircase. Of course, I could not tell whether this was a 66-step or a 166-step staircase. For all I knew, this staircase could have been infinite!

I took three more steps to the *fifteenth* step. As I expected, the waterfall ceased to exist. On the fifteenth step, I heard the sounds of monks praying in a temple. They sang their prayers in soft humming voices. I could hear them all around me, but I could not see anything. I could not understand the words that they uttered as they prayed. A quick count told me once again that there were exactly 66 steps ahead of me.

I then climbed three more steps to the *eighteenth* step. The sound of the monks had stopped, but I could now hear the sounds of the wind as it gently rattled the leaves of palm trees along the ocean shore. I imagined a beautiful beach with pure white sand and a wall of majestic palm trees standing between the beach and the mainland.

I climbed three more steps to the *twenty-first* step. The palm trees had vanished. I could now hear music from one of the finest orchestras that I have ever heard. I could not imagine that such an orchestra could ever exist on this earth. I could not recognise the tune, but I felt most comforted. I did not want this heavenly music to stop!

A few moments later, I climbed up three more steps to the *twenty-fourth* step, where I could now hear the sound of the ocean. The waves crashed against the rocks; it almost sounded as if they were trying to tell me something. The strange thing was that the sounds of the orchestra had *not* stopped. I could still hear the music against the backdrop of the ocean waves. Ahead of me still lay 66 steps.

I then climbed three more steps to the *twenty-seventh* step. I could now hear the strange sound of creatures talking to one another. They sounded like dolphins. I could still hear the waves and the orchestra in the background. "Am I under the ocean?" I asked myself.

Just then I heard the creaking sound of a door opening. I looked up. At the top of the staircase, beyond the 66th step, I could see a door gently opening. Behind this door was a brilliant Light. Normally, when a door opens, you would expect the light behind the door to light up the staircase. Yet this Light only stayed behind the door. It did not illuminate the staircase! "What kind of a Light is this?" I asked myself. "I see It ahead of me, but It does not light up anything that lies outside of the door!" I could still hear the dolphins, the waves and the orchestra. The staircase began to tremble as the sound of thunder came from behind the open door.

In the midst of this thunder, I heard a powerful Voice say to me, *"Welcome to the abode of Eternity. Climb the 66 steps that lie ahead of you and you may step into the land where everything exists in the absence of time. The steps that you have climbed thus far were the steps of time. And you have climbed twenty-seven steps thus far. You have walked through ten Periods or Eras. The first seven Eras were distinct and had a clear break between them. The first seven Eras took you from a marketplace to a dripping tap, to the ticking clock, to children in the playfield, to the waterfall, to the monks in the temple and finally to the palm trees. What is the meaning of these seven distinct Eras? What have they tried to tell you?"*

Bewildered, I said softly, "I do not know what they mean, O Light that stands behind the door."

The Voice replied, *"Think clearly, for you must know what these seven Eras have said to you. Speak your thoughts aloud for all the Eras to hear!"*

"O powerful Light with the Voice of Thunder, what if I am wrong?" I asked.

"If you visited each Era and carefully listened to everything that you have heard, you cannot possibly be wrong," the Voice replied.

"But I could not see anything in each of the seven Eras. All I could hear were sounds," I pleaded.

The Voice replied, *"You were not meant to see anything, for there was nothing to be seen. Everything that was said to you was for you to hear. Now the time has come for you to speak about those Eras. Behold, We are awaiting you!"*

I felt a sense of calmness come over me. My mind flashed back to each Era and then I quietly spoke of what I had learned.

"O Voice of Thunder, when I walked into this building, I was all alone. There was no one with me. Outside the front door of this building was a world that I lived in. I wonder what happened to that world. But, as I looked at this staircase, I knew that this had been the path on which many had trodden. The feet of all the diverse range of people that I saw told me that this staircase had been climbed upon by millions. Did they ever make it to the top? I know not. The marketplace that I heard in the First Era, at the ground floor, was a reaffirmation that many had made this journey before me. I was not the only one. The

First Era was full of life. The marketplace in this Era told me of a world that was truly material, with each person playing his or her role. It was almost like the world that I had left behind me as I entered this building. The First Era, O Voice of Thunder, was indeed a continuation of the material world that I have come from."

The Voice then said, *"You are indeed correct. Now, what did the Second Era tell you?"*

I replied, "There was a distinct break between the First and the Second Era, for no sooner had I stepped up from the First Era, all the sounds of the marketplace ceased to exist. In the Second Era, I heard droplets of water dripping from a tap into a pail with consistent regularity. This to me was a transformation of myself from the crowds of the marketplace to the solitude of a place where only *one* event occurred, which was the dripping of the water. I had moved from multiple events of the First Era to an Era of a singular event. My focus had gone from a broad level down to a narrow level. The significance of the water was the fact that water is the common element in all life forms, from humans to birds, to animals, to plants, to forests, to rivers, to oceans to everything. Hence my focus had narrowed to the slow dripping flow of the 'essence of life', which is water."

The Voice then said, *"You are correct. We are glad to see that you not only recognised the sharpening of your focus, but you also saw through the water as being the essence of life. Therefore, your focus had narrowed down to one of the fundamental ingredients of life. But at this stage, everything is still at a material plane. Now, tell us about the Third Era"*

I continued, "The Third Era was a further transformation, from the seen to the unseen. My focus in the Second Era had narrowed down to water, the essence of life. However, water is an element that can be seen in physical terms. In the Third Era, the ticking of the clock was still a form of singular focus but the time that was represented by the clock was from the unseen. Therefore, the Third Era took me from the plane of the seen to that of the unseen. And in the world of the material, time is the unseen governor of all events."

The Voice then replied, *"You are indeed correct. Each Era has transformed you and you are now at the level of the unseen. Tell us about the Fourth Era now."*

I quietly responded, "The Fourth Era depicted the children in the playground, which signified a new birth for me. I was being transformed into the next phase of my being. This birth was one of joy as portrayed by the happiness of the children in the playground. I was no longer alone, for in that playground there were many children. Hence, this new birth was also one of companionship."

The Voice then said, *"Once again, you are correct. In the Fourth Era, you were reborn with joy and companionship around you. Now, tell us of the Fifth Era."*

I calmly replied, "The Fifth Era was a stage of inner enhancement for me. The flow of the waterfall was a dimension much greater than the dripping of the water from the tap in the Second Era. Water is the essence of life and I was now within an abundant flow of this essence, with all its wonderful energies. Through my new birth in the Fourth Era, I was now granted the essence of life in abundance in the midst of the waterfall. Water that flows rapidly through a river and through waterfalls is naturally pure. Therefore, the Fifth Era also transformed me into a dimension of purity through cleansing by the waterfall."

The Voice then announced, *"The Fifth Era is very significant, for your new birth has taken you into an abundance of essence, together with the purity that must always go with this essence. You are indeed correct. Now you have moved to the Sixth Era. What has it told you?"*

I replied, "The Sixth Era sparked an inner search within me. The temple represents my body. The chanting of the monks signifies my inner voice. And the fact that I can "hear" my inner voice is a symbol of realisation of my inner self. Therefore, the Sixth Era symbolises a realisation of myself. This Era placed me on the path of 'search' for my inner self."

The Voice then said, *"The Sixth Era is the start of a great search. This is a search that does not take you far and wide, but rather takes you deeper and deeper within yourself. You are wise in recognizing that the sound of your inner voice serves as a realisation that there are two dimensions to you. The outer dimension, which is the temple, is your body. The inner dimension is your inner self, of which the Sixth Era has made you aware. You are now moving to the Seventh Era. Tell us about it."*

I replied, "The Seventh Era was my transition to heaven. The palm trees and the pure white sand depict the art and beauty of the Ultimate Creation, which resides in heaven. The gentle rattling of the palm leaves was a sound of complete peace. The energy of the wind added a dimension of strength to this peace. I was being transformed in the Seventh Era to a greater order of strength and peace as I was led towards the beauties of heaven."

The Voice then declared, "*Your new birth has taken you through different stages. After recognizing your inner self in the Sixth Era, you have now begun to experience the strength and peace that resides within you in the Seventh Era. The beauty that surrounds you in this Era can only be ascribed to the highest order of art, which you correctly called heaven.*"

The Voice continued, "*You have learnt a great deal in these seven Eras. Now the Eras that lie ahead of you are no longer separate and distinct. They are interwoven. You have now reached the stage where you can clearly understand what they are telling you. Now you must ponder the Eighth, Ninth, and Tenth Eras and tell us what they mean to you. Remember, once you have crossed the Seventh Era, you are no longer of the material world of finite dimensions. You have taken on a new form, which is a higher form that is not restricted by dimensions. Tell us about the Eighth Era now. And also tell us what has changed between the definite Eras and the less defined Eras. We are listening.*"

I quietly replied, "O Voice of Thunder, I am now undergoing a transition of infinite magnitude. At the end of the Seventh Era, I had achieved ascension to heaven, having gone past distinct and separate Eras of time. I am now like a river that is beginning to merge into the ocean. At the point where the river merges into the ocean, there lies a phase where there is neither the river, nor the ocean. If the water of the river was sweet and the ocean was salty, or each had a separate colour of its own, then where I am as I enter the Eighth Era is the point of meeting of the river and the ocean. At this point one cannot say that I am distinctly in the river or that I am distinctly in the ocean. This is a phase of transition. This is why the next three Eras are not separate and distinct. Each one carries over into the other. This, O Voice of Thunder, is the transition phase of the three Eras that will lead me into the Ultimate Truth."

The Voice replied, *"You have now ascended to a level of knowledge that will lead you to your Origin (Source). On earth, there are signs of this transition phase at points where the rivers meet the oceans. Some rivers flow a long way into the ocean and yet do not merge and become one until the 'Point of Absoluteness' is reached. In The Holy Quran, The Bible, and other Books of Revelations, this phase has been specifically pointed out as a beacon for all creation. The mystics have often wondered why a river does not instantaneously merge into the ocean at the very point that the two meet. This, as you correctly pointed out, is the phase where the Eighth, Ninth and Tenth Eras must be experienced before the 'Point of Absoluteness' is reached. You must now tell us of the Eighth Era; for you have now recognised the transition you are entering."*

Humbled by the depth of this explanation, I quietly replied, "In the Eighth Era, the orchestra plays the music of the heavens. It is a phase or Era of 'harmony' for my soul. The orchestra depicts harmony. Every instrument plays precisely and yet the sound of each instrument blends harmoniously into the others to yield music that can only come from the divine Source. Since my new birth in the Fourth Era, I have undergone transformations and have ascended to the beauties of heaven in the Seventh Era. In the Eighth Era, all the elements of my being are reaching a stage of harmony with one another. And, through this harmony, I am experiencing peace of the highest order. This is the stage of *zero conflict.*"

The Voice then said *"Harmony is an essential aspect of receiving ultimate freedom and enlightenment, for all aspects of your being must be free of conflict. At the stage of complete harmony, all conflicts are gone from within you. Can you ever imagine listening to an orchestra where the instruments are in conflict? It sounds horrible! And yet, in the world of the material, humanity has not refined its hearing to make a distinction between the music of conflict and that of harmony. It is only at the Eighth Era that true harmony is experienced within your inner self. Now, you are going to the Ninth Era. Tell us what you have learnt."*

In complete humility, I replied, "In the Ninth Era, the sounds of the ocean signify my ascension to the level of Totality. The ocean represents Totality and the water in the ocean represents the Essence of Totality. All droplets, rivers, lakes and streams ultimately enter the ocean where they achieve totality. In the Ninth Era, I have ascended into Totality. The distinction between me and Totality is non-existent for I am now Totality itself."

The Voice then said, *"You have risen to a level in the Ninth Era where the singular identity of your self has now merged into the total. And, the total is indeed pure unity. In an ocean, all the water that has travelled from everywhere merges to form one united ocean that can never be divisible anymore. You have now merged into total unity. And remember that you are still in the transition stage of the last three Eras. Therefore, your unity now bears complete harmony, because all aspects of unity are harmonious in nature."*

The Voice continued, *"You are now stepping into the Tenth Era, which is the final Era before the 66 steps to the Light of the Universe. What have you learned from this Era?"*

I quietly and humbly replied, "In the Tenth Era I hear creatures talking within the ocean. They sound like dolphins, who are inhabitants of the ocean. They represent the voice of the Ocean. The Tenth Era, O Voice of Thunder, is the inner voice of Totality. When I heard my inner voice in the Sixth Era, it was a realisation of myself. But now that I have merged into Totality, the Tenth Era is for me a realisation of the inner voice of Totality."

The Voice then said, *"You have reached the highest level of the Ten Eras. Yes, indeed, the dolphins signify the voice of the ocean, just as the monks signified the voice of the temple. Now, for you the temple no longer exists for you are the ocean. Hence, the voice of the ocean has now become you, for you are totality. And you are now leaving the phase of transition for you have achieved harmony, unity, and realisation of totality. Beyond the Tenth Era lie the 66 steps, which will lead you through the door of Light, where you will achieve union with the Light. You will then become Light yourself."*

The Voice continued, *"You may climb each of the 66 steps, one at a time. You are now in harmony with the Light that you can see, and each step from here will totalise this harmony. You are free of all conflicts. Rise and ascend, for the door of Light awaits you."*

I slowly climbed the stairs, one at a time, until I reached the last step before the door. The Voice then said, *"You have climbed the 66 steps and are at the doorstep to the Light of the Universe. As you step in, you will become Light. Herein ends your journey, for you have merged into the ocean; you have reached the Point of Absoluteness. Beyond this point, you are no longer the river. You are united with the ocean. This is the ocean of Light. This is the ultimate level that all souls seek to reach. But only the ones that are blessed will reach this ocean of Light and gain enlightenment."*

As I stepped through the door and entered the Light, I heard the words, *"You are now no longer you. That is your fulfillment...."*

The "Sixty-Six Steps" describes a mystical spiritual journey. As we read about each of the ten stages, we should carefully and deeply reflect upon the symbols and events that are portrayed at each stage. This will assist us to recognise at what stage we are at in our own spiritual journey.

The Eight Era, the level of the orchestra, is the most difficult stage of the entire journey. This is the stage of total harmony, where all the instruments of the orchestra are in complete unison with one another. There is no conflict, for even if only one of the instruments were not in tune, the music of perfection would not manifest. The Eight Era is the level of *zero conflict*. The Voice of Thunder said that this is the level that most cannot transcend, for achieving zero conflict is indeed the greatest challenge of all. It was the Eighth Era that inspired me to write this book, with the view to defining conflict, in its fundamental dimensions, and sharing methods by which we can identify and overcome all our conflicts. As we draw from the Seeds of Resolution, described at the end of the preceding chapters, and rise above our conflicts, we may find that all the instruments of our orchestra will begin to play in unison, until the level of ultimate harmony is reached.

After the Tenth Era, the era of the dolphins, I was allowed to ascend the 66 steps to the door of the Light. This Light was the ultimate destination of my soul's journey. As I stepped through the door into the Light, I heard the words, *"Now you are no longer you. That is your fulfilment."*

I had merged with the Light of Oneness. Thereafter, it became apparent to me that all living things have their roots in this Oneness. All living things draw their life energy from this Oneness. When I looked outward from the Oneness, I saw creatures take physical form through birth and drop their physical form through death. I recognised that every living thing has its roots in the Oneness. It was now clear to me that this earth and all its life forms, as well as the universe and all its life forms, are indeed a part of one great Unity. I realised that we are closer to one another than we think. The only thing that separates us from each other is our physical body. We are all truly an integral part of one another. We are all rays of the Light of Oneness. This was a most beautiful realisation, which taught me that, *"Through the Oneness, I am you and you are me. Together we are everything."* This is the statement of universal truth that I had now fully understood. If we are all indeed one, how could we possibly want to harm one another? By harming a fellow being, we would actually be harming ourselves. This statement of universal truth is the source or basis for the Ten Commandments and all the other prescribed codes of living taught by the world's great religions.

I also learned from this experience that each one of us embodies a great deal more power than we realise. We are not as helpless as we sometimes think we are. Our roots lie within the Light of Creation, which enables us to access energies of creation, healing and ultimate intelligence. Meditation is a tool through which we can access and harness these energies.

MEDITATION, AN INVALUABLE TOOL

In order to experience the Oneness, we must pass the stage of *zero conflict*. In the process, we transcend many of our human weaknesses and rise to a level where we are completely open to achieving Oneness. Meditation is a very helpful tool in this process.

There are many different kinds of meditation that one can practise. In previous chapters, I shared with you certain guided meditations that can be used as tools for self-development and overcoming inner conflict. However, for those who wish to progress spiritually, there is another kind of meditation that can be practised for spiritual development. This meditation involves creation of alignment of the body, mind and life energy (or Higher Self). Below is a brief description of how this meditation can be practised. It is important to recognise that people of *all* religions and walks of life can practise this meditation, as it is completely universal in nature.

MEDITATION OF ONENESS

The Meditation of Oneness (see Note at the end of this chapter) is based on focusing the body, mind and life energy (Higher Self) upon the Source of all creation. Before starting this meditation, you need to select a name that you wish to associate with your Source. It should be a name that you are personally most comfortable with. Some choose a name for the Source that may be in accordance with their personal or religious beliefs, such as, God, Bhagwaan, Father, Dios, Allah, Origin, Nature, etc. Selecting any name is fine because this meditation can be practised at a personal, religious or universal level, depending upon what you are most comfortable with.

As in all meditation practises, it is best to sit quietly and comfortably in a place with minimal distractions, close your eyes, and breathe freely in order to relax the body and mind. The position of the body is not important. You may select any position that avoids bodily discomfort in order to minimise distractions caused by an uncomfortable posture.

Once you have relaxed your body and mind, start to focus your attention on your Source, which is Oneness. Imagine that you are watching all the rays of the sun travelling backwards and merging back into the core of the sun. Observe this unifying process carefully as it occurs in your mind. Once all the rays have merged, what is left is the core of the sun, which is Light and Oneness. Once you have reached this point, you may start to repeat within your mind the name that you have chosen for your Source. Focus on this word and repeat it very slowly in your mind. Try to "hear" it within yourself rather than "say" it. Continue to focus on this word for as long as you can maintain your concentration. Some days, you may be able to focus for only one minute and other days, you may be able to concentrate for an hour. The duration of the meditation is not important. The quality of concentration is what matters the most.

If, during your meditation, you lose focus, then return to the thought of all the rays of the sun travelling back to the sun until no more rays can be seen. All that remains is the core of the sun, which is a Light of Unity or Oneness. Once you have regained this focus, you may continue to repeat the name of your Source very calmly and slowly.

You may stop the meditation whenever you wish. Normally, you would feel calm and relaxed by the end of the process. Sometimes, you may find yourself experiencing new feelings during the meditation, such as those you have never experienced before. The best thing to do at such times is to *let it be* and go with the flow, wherever this experience takes you. At other times, you may feel absolutely nothing during your meditation. That is okay too because the experience of the Oneness that you are seeking lies beyond the comprehension of the human mind. The Oneness can only be experienced. It cannot be imagined or described, for there is no vocabulary in our material world that can describe something which has an infinite number of dimensions, and each of the dimensions is itself infinite.

The Meditation of Oneness is a passive process. It is a process of waiting and listening. It is like tuning a radio until the right channel is found. In this meditation, you need to be patient and remain open to experiencing the Oneness (Unity). You should not try to actively imagine anything, or to think too much about your feelings or about how well you are or are not concentrating. These are unimportant matters. The important thing is to open yourself to receiving self-recognition and experiencing pure Unity (Oneness). It is like going to the cinema. It does not matter what position you sit in or how you breathe. It does not matter how hard you try to imagine what the movie will be like. Only by fully engaging in watching the movie are you able to "receive" the story.

The quieter our minds become, the more open we become to gaining clarity and meaning from our meditation. *Silence, stillness and passive listening from within* are essential elements for success in meditation. Have you ever tried speaking to the screen while trying to watch a movie? Obviously, you cannot speak and hear the story at the same time! Similarly in meditation, we need to silence the mind, like making the choppy waters of a lake become still. You cannot see your face or reflection in choppy waters. But, when the waters become completely still, you can see your image in the water with total clarity. This is how meditation works. When we recognise ourselves, we recognise the Oneness, as we are an integral part of Oneness.

Many people tend to expect too much too quickly from meditation. If they cannot concentrate for more than a few minutes, they get very disappointed and then give up the meditation. Remember, meditation is a timeless search for the Oneness within you. Pure concentration that lasts one minute is more meaningful than an hour of struggle to concentrate. The best approach to Meditation of Oneness is to sit in stillness, open yourself to gaining the experience that you are seeking and then go with the flow. Apart from spiritual development, this meditation provides relaxation that comes from allowing the mind to take a break. This helps to enhance your mental capacities, control your emotions and achieve success in all dimensions of your life.

Practising the Meditation of Oneness daily is recommended, especially at a time when you have completed all your duties of the day, for example just before bedtime or soon after you awake in the morning. Some people prefer to awake at the early hours of dawn to perform their meditation as the world is at its most tranquil state at that time.

Daily meditation for a few minutes, together with a constant recognition that we are all part of Oneness, our Source, will help us a great deal to eliminate conflict from within us, through inner peace.

Note: I have produced a set of audio tapes and CDs, which teach meditation in a simple and easily understandable form, to people of all ages. They include guided meditations that help to build physical and mental focus, while paving the way for a journey of self-realisation. I recommend the use of these tapes and CDs since they provide excellent tools for self-development and achievement of a higher level of understanding about life and its purpose. They cover the process and mechanics of meditation at a level that is much deeper than that presented in this chapter. To order these, please see the information at the back of the book.

Seeds of Resolution

❀ Let us contemplate and internalise the following seeds:

"I AM NEVER ALONE

FOR I AM PART OF ONENESS.

I AM PART OF EVERYTHING."

❀ These words have a soothing energy of their own that help to remind us how close we are to one another.

❀ They remind us that we have no room for conflict within us.

❀ They help us build ourselves from within so that we may be able to transcend the Era of the orchestra, which is, in fact, the most challenging stage in our journey.

❀ Beyond this Era, we can ultimately reach and enter through the door at the end of the 66 steps and merge into Oneness, the final destination that we should all strive to reach.

❀ That will be the ultimate fulfilment of our timeless journey.

My Reflections

Now   date: /   /   .

My Reflections

One Year Hence   date: /   /   .

My Reflections

Chapter 17

HARMONY

One Saturday morning, Alex, a long-distance runner who represented Great Britain in the Olympics, went out for his daily training jog in the beautiful Yorkshire Moors. Alex loved taking long, steady runs through the fields and the hills. Whilst he obviously got his physical exercise in this way each day, it also gave him an opportunity to reflect upon and contemplate important matters in his life. Alex found the joy of being with nature truly inspiring.

As he began a brisk walk that preceded his run, he thought to himself, "Today I am going to look for harmony in the Moors."

Alex had heard and read much about harmony and today he wanted to set out to discover the meaning of this fascinating word. As he started to run, he began to repeat the word "harmony" in each breath that he took. This was Alex' way of focusing on the issues that he wanted to reflect upon.

After running for about 30 minutes, Alex stopped at a chain link fence and began to look carefully at it. Every link came together perfectly and the sum total of these linkages formed the fence, which Alex could see, had strength of its own. He asked himself, "Do I see harmony in this chain link fence?"

As he reflected upon this question, he began to realise that all the links did come together with perfection, to give form and strength to the fence. He nodded his head as he recognised that harmony indeed existed in this fence, in a very simple form.

As Alex continued with his run, his mind drifted to a recent book he had read on contemporary art, where the concept of harmony was discussed with respect to colours, shapes and forms. The book talked about the blending of colours in a harmonious, non-conflicting manner, to create images that were soothing for the eyes. The word "blending" struck a chord in Alex' mind. Clearly, various colours needed to come together for this blending to occur. Once they came together, they projected their own unique feelings and emotions that could be sensed by the artist and his or her audience. If the blend was comprised of colours that complemented and enhanced one another, the image took on a soothing and meaningful expression. This blend had to have colours that did not conflict with one another.

On the other hand, conflicting colours could also be put together. Images painted with these colours would be harsh, revealing different dimensions of conflict in a symbolic form. Alex recognised that in order to have harmony in a painting, the blend of colours had to be put together in the absence of conflict. In addition, all the colours that made up the painting had to be present, for even one colour missing could leave a painful void in the picture, giving rise to an image that did not appeal to the eye of the viewer.

As he thought further, he realised that harmony was an essential aspect of art and yet, the work of art had to have all its components (colours), blended in such a way that they were free of conflict.

For Alex, the chain link fence represented a very simple form of harmony. The only component of the fence was the links, which came together in a simple, organised manner. The concept of harmony in art offered a broader dimension for Alex to reflect upon, from colours and their blends, to shapes, to forms and their respective patterns.

Alex had been running now for almost an hour and he had been able to focus most of his attention on harmony. He was beginning to understand it better. A few minutes later, Alex stopped at his favourite lake and began to look intently at the little ripples of water that glittered in the bright sunlight. Each ripple rose and subsided in the water with a precise frequency. He marvelled at the fact that each ripple was a replica of its predecessor.

The whole lake was alive with these ripples, which reflected the sunlight as beautiful little flashes that made the lake look like it was communicating with some distant planet in the universe!

Alex looked at the ripples and said to himself, "Here is harmony again, but this time it is in motion. The ripples follow each other with absolute precision and regularity. Their motion carries harmony. As the ripples travel, they reflect the sunlight with equal regularity. This lake represents harmony."

Alex had now recognised the presence of harmony in motion. He remembered his physics lessons at school where he learnt about waves, their frequency and amplitude. He had learnt about the harmonious actions of such waves, as each cycle of the wave followed its predecessor in a pure, complementary fashion.

After an energetic three-hour jog, Alex arrived back at his home in the village of Yarm. That evening, he went to a classical music concert with his girlfriend, Lynda. Alex loved watching live orchestras perform the works of the world's greatest composers. This evening's special feature was Beethoven, Alex' favourite composer. Alex found himself drifting into the music, chord-by-chord, and beat-by-beat. Every instrument of the orchestra played its part with perfection. Then came the chorus that brought some 24 human voices together in perfect unison with every instrument of the orchestra.

For Alex, this was the music of perfection. It was the music of the heavens. The soul of this blissful music lay in the harmony. This was the ultimate demonstration for Alex of the power and beauty of harmony. He watched each musician and singer perform with pure energy and total synchronisation, which bestowed complete harmony to the music. This orchestra was delivering a music that had *zero conflict*. It was pure and perfect. It had infinite energy and endless possibilities, with respect to the messages and feelings it was conveying.

Alex wondered, "What would happen if one of the musicians stopped playing their instrument? What would happen if even one of the instruments were no longer coordinated with the rest of the orchestra? How would the music sound?" As he pondered these questions, the player of the flute suddenly made a mistake and missed a few notes. His tune was not synchronised with the rest of the instruments for a short time. Alex immediately recognised that he could hear the flute in isolation from the rest of the orchestra. The sound of the flute now was in conflict with the orchestra. The music had lost its perfection. The one instrument that caused the loss of harmony stood out on its own rather like a sore thumb. As the remainder of the musicians and the conductor attempted to rectify this mistake, the pianist lost his tune. The music got worse and the conflict spread quickly through the orchestra. It took one single instrument, the flute, to destroy the music that had reached perfection. It took one single instrument to spread its conflict to the piano, which was the heart of the composition, and thereafter to an utter and absolute chaos!

The conductor stopped the music and allowed the musicians to realign themselves. A few moments later, the orchestra was playing once again with full force. Every instrument was in complete harmony with the rest of the orchestra. Every voice in the chorus was also in complete harmony. Once again, the orchestra was delivering the music of perfection. It took a process of realignment to restore the harmony of the orchestra.

Alex had learned a great deal about harmony that day, from a simple chain link fence, to paintings, to ripples in the lake and now, finally, to a complete orchestra!

When we think about achieving *zero conflict*, we need to consider every element that causes conflict in our lives as being equivalent to an instrument in an orchestra. These include, for example, jealousy, hatred, oppression, being judgemental, criticism, anger, rigidity, intervention, etc. Our aim should be to recognise each conflict, correct it and manage it in a manner that allows the instrument that it represents, to become a positive, harmonious participant in the orchestra of our life. We should remember that each one of us is the conductor of his or her own orchestra. The role of the conductor is to ensure that every instrument comes together (like colours that blend in a painting) in a totally coordinated fashion (like the ripples in the lake), with pure simplicity (like the chain link fence), to yield a harmony that delivers the music of perfection, joy, power and pure energy in our lives.

As we achieve this harmony, we come closer to the state of *zero conflict*, where we become pure energy ourselves; where our potential becomes infinite; where our possibilities are endless; and where our true strength, our Light, and our powers begin to manifest in each and every breath that we take. This is the state where we will be able to experience true peace, love, happiness, and Oneness with the Source of our life, our Origin; and Oneness with our fellow beings and with all creation. From hereon, we will be on the path to success and enlightenment. Remember the journey of the "Sixty-Six Steps" in Chapter 16? The Voice of Thunder said that the Eighth Era, the level of the orchestra and *zero conflict*, is the most difficult hurdle of all to cross. It is the level at which most fail to transcend. Once *zero conflict* has been achieved, the ascension to Oneness, through the Ninth and Tenth Eras (the levels of the ocean and the dolphins) can be rapid. Hence, as we begin to achieve *zero conflict*, our path to enlightenment opens up before our eyes, for we are then like the river that is merging into the ocean.

Achieving *zero conflict* will also bring us peace, happiness, contentment and the true experience of love that we can draw upon and give to all those around us. The lessons presented in this book are like the golden keys that open the doors of peace, happiness, success and Light in every aspect of our lives. After all, with these keys firmly embedded in our minds, heart and soul, *zero conflict* becomes a natural component of each and every step of our life's journey!

Seeds of Resolution

It would be appropriate to conclude this book with a meditation as the Seed of Resolution. *It is called the* Meditation of the Orchestra. *The aim of this meditation is to help us to bring together all the elements of our being, into a state of pure harmony.*
(This meditation is also available
on audio tape and CD).

MEDITATION OF THE ORCHESTRA.

❀ Find a comfortable sitting or resting position, close your eyes and relax. This is a meditation about an orchestra.

❀ Imagine that you are sitting in a crowded theatre, watching and listening to an orchestra that is producing the music of perfection. The stage is well lit and all the instruments are shining before your eyes. The players of the instruments are spread out evenly across the stage. Behind them, on a higher platform, stands a choir of young men and women dressed in colourful robes. The conductor stands before the orchestra and waves his or her stick, directing each player with precision and discipline.

❀ It is now time for each player to give a solo performance.
❀ The bass violin begins to play. It produces a deep sound that represents strong foundations. As you listen to this

instrument, you see before you the earth, with endless fields and plains, which are indeed the foundations upon which all living things grow and live. Take a few moments and look at the fields and the plains.

❀ Next, the harp begins to play, yielding an enchanting music of flow. You see before you mountains with rivers flowing down them, sending crystal clear water towards the valleys. Watch this scene and absorb its colours and beauty.

❀ Now the piano takes its turn, with tunes of youth and playfulness. You see before you waves in a lake, dancing playfully before your eyes. They reflect the sunlight with power and radiance, amidst pure harmony. Look at this spectacle of nature.

❀ Then, the cellos (small violins) begin to play, yielding sounds of energy and life. You see before you dolphins dancing in unison in the sea, jumping with freedom, in a rhythmic order. Look at these beautiful creatures.

❀ Next, you hear the clarinet, which conveys music of grace and tranquillity. You see before you butterflies, fluttering their wings, displaying an amazing array of colours that can only come from heaven. Enjoy the peace that they bring to you.

❀ Now, the drums begin, bringing forth the sound of thunder from the skies. You see before you endless dark clouds, pouring rain upon the thirsty earth. This is the rain of nourishment and generosity. Listen to the powerful sound of the drums and look at the rain as it rushes from the skies to kiss the earth.

* The chorus comes on next, bringing music from the finest instrument in the universe — the human voice. The chorus blesses the orchestra with unity and perfection. You see before you a rainbow that has now broken through the rain clouds, standing majestically against the sun. The rainbow ties the earth together from horizon to horizon. Its colours blend perfectly into one another, displaying unity in its purest form. Take a few moments to cherish this rainbow that links the earth from end to end.

* Finally, the flute begins to play, yielding music of the divine. This is the music of the heavens, to which the angels dance, amidst the Light of the Universe. You see before you beautiful, white doves, flapping their wings in the Light, bringing you an experience of pure freedom and bliss. Watch the doves as they fly away from you into the Light until you can see them no more.

* Now that each member of the orchestra has played a solo, the conductor makes a gesture for all to play together. All the musicians and the chorus unite to take this concert to a new height.

* All you can now see is Light. A Light that is warm, loving and peaceful. The whole stage has filled up with Light and all the instruments are playing with full harmony, power and grace. Everything has come alive and the entire orchestra has become a pool of life, amidst the

Light. Look at this scene of power and absorb the life that it brings to your soul.

❋ Your eyes now focus on the conductor standing before you, conducting the orchestra with precision in the core of this divine Light. Slowly, the conductor turns around to face you.

❋ You smile as you recognise this face, for it is non other than your own face.

❋ You are now above all conflict...

My Reflections

Now   date: /   /   .

My Reflections

One Year Hence   date: /   /   .

TOWARDS ZERO CONFLICT AUDIO TOOLS

This book contains important contemplations in the form of Seeds of Resolution, which require focused attention. Sometimes, it is easier to listen to these contemplations in the form of audio recordings, because such recordings allow you to sit back, relax and focus on their essence.

There are also a number of important guided meditations in this book, which have a deeper meaning when we listen to them, rather than read them. The voice recordings of each meditation permit you to follow the flow of the meditation without any external distractions. In this way, you will be able to derive greater benefit from the inner learning process.

As a result, we have prepared an audio CD and cassette, entitled, *"Towards Zero Conflict - Seeds of Resolution and Guided Meditations"* (ISBN 1-9044281-4-2 for CD's and ISBN 1-9044281-3-4 for cassettes). You may obtain them from your local bookshop or at **www.amyndahya.com.**

ABOUT THE AUTHOR

Amyn Dahya is an internationally acclaimed scientist, author and personal development teacher, who produces works of inspiration in the form of parables and insights, that articulate complex concepts about our material and spiritual lives, in a simple form that can be understood by people of all ages, cultures and walks of life.

He travels extensively around the world, sharing his inspirations in the form of motivational books, lectures, seminars and workshops. He also teaches people to heal themselves through meditation, by enabling them to tap into their inner reservoir of creative and healing energies. To date, he has helped thousands of people on a voluntary basis, to heal themselves from a broad range of physical, mental and emotional ailments.

Amyn Dahya's writings foster a special bond between the reader and his or her inner self, thus creating an understanding of the message that is being conveyed, at a deep, personal level. This has been the experience of readers of his books all over the world.

BOOKS AND LECTURES BY AMYN DAHYA

BOOKS:

❋ Reflections from the Origin
ISBN 0-9682683-1-5

❋ Parables from the Origin
ISBN 0-9682683-2-3

❋ Towards Zero Conflict
ISBN 1-9044281-1-8

❋ Be and It Is
ISBN 1-9044280-8-8

❋ Sea y asi Será (Spanish)
ISBN 1-9044280-9-6

LECTURES (AUDIO TAPES & CDs)

❋ Meditation 1 - Alignment of the Body and Intellect
ISBN 1-9044280-1-0 (CD)
ISBN 1-9044280-2-9 (Cassette)

❋ Meditation 2 - The Spiritual Journey
ISBN 1-9044280-0-2 (CD)
ISBN 1-9044280-3-7 (Cassette)

❋ Limitless Horizons - The Purpose of Life
ISBN 1-9044281-2-6 (CD)
ISBN 1-9044281-3-4 (Cassette)

❀ Towards Zero Conflict
Seeds of Resolution and Guided Meditations
ISBN 1-9044281-4-2 (CD)
ISBN 1-9044281-5-0 (Cassette)

❀ Towards Zero Conflict - Audio Book
ISBN 1-9044281-6-9 (CD)
ISBN 1-9044281-7-7 (Cassette)

❀ Reflections from the Origin - Audio Book
ISBN 1-9044281-8-5 (CD)
ISBN 1-9044281-9-3 (Cassette)

❀ Parables from the Origin - Audio Book
ISBN 1-9044282-0-7 (CD)
ISBN 1-9044282-1-5 (Cassette)

Empowered Living Publications

Pol. Industrial, Segunda Fase, 72-BIS
Alhaurin de la Torre
Malaga, CP 29130, Spain

Tel. Spain: 34-952 411 439
Tel. UK: 44-7817 779 109

Email: info@amyndahya.com

Website: www.amyndahya.com